GW00982561

IRISH LOVE POEMS

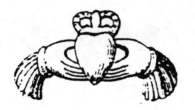

Ex Libris

IRISH LOVE POEMS

Edited by A. Norman Jeffares

THE O'BRIEN PRESS
DUBLIN

Irish American Book Company (IABC)
Boulder, Colorado

This book is dedicated to John and Felicity Riddy.

First published 1997 by The O'Brien Press Ltd.,
20 Victoria Road, Dublin 6, Ireland

Published in the US and Canada by the Irish American Book Company (IABC)
6309 Monarch Park Place, Suite 101, Niwot, Colorado 80503
Office: Tel. 303-652-2710 Fax. 303-652-2689
Orders: Tel. 800-452-7115 Fax. 800-401-9705

2 3 4 5 6 7 8 9 10
98 99 00 01 02 03 04 05 06

British Library Cataloguing in Publication Data
Jeffares, A. Norman (Alexander Norman), 1920-
Irish Love Poems
1. English poetry – Irish authors 2. Love poetry, English
I. Title
821.9'14'08'03543

ISBN 0-86278-514-6

The O'Brien Press receives assistance from The Arts Council/An Chomhairle Ealaíon

Cover: 'Nude Against Stormy Seascape' by Roderic O'Conor,
courtesy of the Estate of Roderic O'Conor

Typesetting: The O'Brien Press Ltd
Design: John Power
Cover design: The O'Brien Press Ltd
Cover separations: Lithoset Ltd
Printing: Guernsey Press Ltd

CONTENTS

FRUSTRATION AND JEALOUSY

WOMEN

MARRIAGE

LAMENTATIONS

PARTINGS AND RETURNINGS

CELEBRATIONS

PLEASURE

THE SUPERNATURAL

YOUTH, AGE AND MEMORY

O ver the centuries Irish love poetry has taken on many forms: these range between the realistic and the romantic, the idealistic and the satiric, and the tragic and the comic. Love poetry is a convenient catch-all title to cover the variety, the simplicities or the intricate intensities of the human relationships involved. This anthology includes, then, poems dealing with such themes as initiations of love, flirtations and courtships, praise and devotion, encounters, togetherness, frustration and jealousy, women, marriage, lamentations, partings and returnings, celebrations, pleasure, the supernatural, youth, age and memory. Within each of these groupings the poems have been arranged in chronological order of poet.

Some poets rejoice fearlessly in love without reservation while others can play safe by undercutting; others, again, praise the beloved or lament failure to achieve or maintain love's rapport. The variety seems infinite. An anthology can but offer love poems which seem memorable and enjoyable, and for different reasons: the force of passion given lasting literary life; equally violent melancholia or despair; noble or even wry praise celebrating the honesty, steadfastness and bravery which inspire committed devotion. There is also awareness of how the lover can be under the power of someone attractive but unworthy. Wit keeps breaking in, sometimes at the service of the lover's desire to create a persuasive argument, but very occasionally because it seems to have an impish life of its own wedded to the ridiculous. Paradoxically perhaps, lightheartedness can add to a poem's validity. Ultimately, however, it is the power of imagination that infuses love poetry with its effective intensity. Initial inspiration may not be enough: successful love poetry demands a shaping skill, the craft of the poet.

In Irish life the poet has had an influential position, from the heroic phase on through Old and Middle Irish into the period – about 1200 to 1600 – when two aristocratic cultures, Gaelic and Norman Gaelic, blended polished, courtly love poetry, the bards employing traditional metric forms. With the collapse of the Gaelic civilisation in the 17th century poets bereft of aristocratic patronage moved from traditional, ornate, elegant and tightly ordered metrical formats into a use of assonance, into song. Poetry composed in Irish survived in schools of poetry scattered about the country. The consequent change in style led to more directness in love poems, more simplicity, a more spontaneous expression. The genre of the love vision, the *Aisling*, became popular in

the 18th century. It celebrated a female persona, representing Ireland,
blending praise of a beautiful woman or fairy woman with a political
prophecy of Ireland rescued by a Stuart prince (Mangan's 'Dark
Rosaleen' belongs to this kind of amatory-political poetry).

Poems written in English by Swift and his contemporaries in the
18th century were mainly shaped by neo-classical attitudes, the drama-
tists contributing elegant love songs. But an awakening interest in anti-
quarianism in the latter part of the century turned attention to Irish
music and poetry. Joseph Cooper Walker's *Historical Memoirs of the Irish
Bards* appeared in 1786, and the influence of Charlotte Brooke's trans-
lations, *Reliques of Irish Poetry* (1789), was widespread in what was vir-
tually a re-discovery by English speakers and writers of the language,
the customs and the culture of Gaelic Ireland. Edward Bunting's
impressive *A General Collection of the Ancient Music of Ireland* appeared
in editions of 1796, 1809 and 1840. Thomas Moore's poetry owed much
to Bunting's work and to his friend Edward Hudson, a flautist who col-
lected Irish airs. Moore had an ability to control his natural fluency and
his songs on Irish themes have a fluid insouciant ease. Possessed of a
fine voice, he had also a sure sense of metre. He wanted to charm, to
make popular songs and he succeeded: the limpid plangency of his *Irish
Melodies* continues to echo: they can sometimes seem sentimental but
they remain effective, vibrantly emotive.

After Moore came translators and adaptors of Irish love poetry:
those who gathered round Sir George Petrie in the days of the
Ordnance Survey (from 1832 to 1842) included Eugene O'Curry, and
James Clarence Mangan. Sir Samuel Ferguson produced vivid verse
translations which caught the narrative power and energy of Irish folk
song. Ferguson was one of the influences confirming the youthful W.B.
Yeats in his determination to become an Irish poet of a new kind, in his
desire to present Irish material in a new way. Yeats knew no Irish, but
intense reading of Gaelic mythology and legend was combined with his
love of the local places, traditions, stories and songs, found in the Sligo
of his childhood; his love poetry, however, was stimulated by his obses-
sion with Maud Gonne, for whom he wrote delicate, dreamy, devoted
love poems in the 1890s. This was poetry concerned with beauty,
increasingly permeated with a deliberate, esoteric symbolism, adjectival
and affected by his studies of the occult, Pre-Raphaelitism and French
Symbolism. It set the tone for many of his contemporaries in the literary
movement sometimes called, after one of his books, *The Celtic Twilight*.
Subsequently, however, at the turn of the century when, as he put it,
everyone got down off their stilts, his poetry began to embrace an

outspoken treatment of sex, incorporated into the vigorous flowering of his middle and late poetry.

While Yeats was working hard creating literary societies, writing articles and reviews on Irish literature in order to create a cultural revival in the early 1890s, Douglas Hyde was equally involved in preserving and translating Irish oral traditions in poems and stories. As founding President of the Gaelic League in 1893 and President of the Irish Literary Society, he stressed the need to de-Anglicise Ireland. His *Love Songs of Connacht* appeared that year, combining his scholarship and creativity, and conveying convincingly the emotional strength of the originals he had collected. His contemporary Eleanor Hull, founder of the Irish Texts Society, and Kuno Meyer, the German scholar, continued this work. Lady Gregory, whose main effort went into her fine translations of the Ulster and Fenian cycles, also translated Irish love poems, employing colloquialism to make them more accessible. Other poets proved themselves effective translators, among them James Stephens and Joseph Campbell. Robin Flower and Frank O'Connor brought their visions of older Irish love poetry into fresh and sharp focus, something continued by recent translators, often poets distinguished for their own original poetry: Thomas Kinsella, Brendan Kennelly, Eileán ní Chuilleanáin, Michael Hartnett, Paul Durcan, Gabriel Fitzmaurice and Nuala ní Dhomhnaill.

Yeats did much to attack the sentimental rhetoric prevalent in his youth (some of it, however, particularly in ballads and songs, can still be appealing). At the turn of the century his increasingly robust attitudes helped to replace Ireland's 19th-century respectability with more direct utterance, to free Irish love poetry from the web of delicate tracery with which he had himself bound it in the days of the Celtic Twilight. A move towards modernism in the twenties and thirties pushed the balance well away from romanticism, although the puritanism of the new Irish Free State was not very conducive to it. So love poetry between the twenties and forties seems to exist in individual, ungrouped – almost isolated – outputs, poets publishing in journals because publishing books of poetry in Ireland presented problems. These began to be solved with the establishment of the Dolmen Press by Liam Miller in 1951, which harboured a new generation of poets.

With the sixties came new publishers and a new outspokenness, particularly in love poems written by women. There had been much strong feeling in women's poems since the twenties but it was often to be discovered below the surface. Now that a general freedom of expression prevails, a new equality of honesty sometimes makes it difficult –

and unnecessary – to know the sex of the poet, love being, after all, a shared experience: shared according to the varying nature of those who experience and write about it. The ideal equality of emotion often varies between dominance and compliance and is affected by approaches or retreats, pursuits or rejections. So there is an interplay – love and hatred, delight and disillusion – and Irish love poetry as a result is rich in diversity.

This directness was there in Gaelic poetry. Men were not automatically dominant in, say, the 9th century and amorous advances were often made by women. Deirdre and Gráinne are good examples of this, while Maeve was a queen who could fight successfully and was generous, demanding of Ailill as a husband that he be a man without meanness, jealousy or fear. The old Gaelic Brehon laws gave women many rights, including divorce. But Christianity, inevitably, produced changes; the church's law incorporated attitudes very different from those of the older Brehon code, though the early Irish church was liberal in its treatment, for instance, of celibacy. Medieval anti-feminism had an effect (and signs of this recur in later poetry): a male desire for independence, part of the concept of the sex war, could prompt such sentiments as 'I will not Die for You' against which, of course, we can set the complaints of women against celibacy in Brian Merriman's exuberantly comic *The Midnight Court* with its enthusiastic celebration of sexuality.

The *amour courtois* flourishing between the 13th and 16th centuries had elements which carried on into popular Irish poetry. Direct expressions of sexual love, however, tended to be swamped by a general sense of propriety, often confused with morality in the 18th and, especially, 19th centuries. Now we are back to the personal frankness and irony again in both English and Irish love poetry, and it is refreshing, for, however much a love poem may use or react against the poetic conventions of its time, it remains a supremely individual statement.

A. Norman Jeffares
Fife Ness, 1997

INTIMATIONS

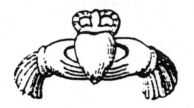

THOMAS MOORE (1779-1852)

The Kiss

Give me, my love, that billing kiss
　　I taught you one delicious night,
When, turning epicures in bliss,
　　We tried inventions of delight.

Come, gently steal my lips along,
　　And let your lips in murmurs move –
Ah, no! – again – that kiss was wrong –
　　How can you be so dull, my love?

'Cease, cease!' the blushing girl replied –
　　And in her milky arms she caught me –
'How can you thus your pupil chide;
　　You know 'twas in the dark you taught me!'

FERGUS ALLEN (b 1921)

Age Twelve

Eating rashers and beans
In Woolworth's cafeteria,
Thinking of three-speed gears
Or perhaps of James Stewart
(Certainly not of you,
Rusticated for Lent
In the drizzle and pasture
Of County Carlow's farmland),
I saw you at the counter,
Sliding your tray along,
Not in your dark green gymslip
But a cable-stitch jumper
And not too modest skirt.

Laid-back today, ironic,
I live with unsurprises,
But then my heart, no, diaphragm,
Was jolted from below
As if a whale had surfaced
In waters off Cape Clear,
Showed its encrusted flanks
And slowly resubmerged
Into a flux of foam –
Undreamt-of elemental
Making its presence felt.

I was unseen, invisible,
Anything to avert
The artificial lightning
And removal of bandages.
Time enough for the first steps
On stiff legs in the laboratory.

DEREK MAHON (b 1941)

The Lost Girls *from* Autobiographies

'In ancient shadows and twilights
Where childhood had strayed'
I ran round in the playground
Of Skegoneill Primary School
During the lunch hour,
Pretending to be a plane.

For months I would dawdle home
At a respectful distance
Behind the teacher's daughter,
Eileen Boyd, who lived
In a house whose back garden
Was visible from my window.

I watched her on summer evenings,
A white dress picking flowers,
Her light, graceful figure
Luminous and remote.
We never exchanged greetings:
Her house was bigger than ours.

She married an older man
And went to live in Kenya.
Perhaps she is there still
Complaining about 'the natives'.
It would be nice to know;
But who can re-live their lives?

Eileen Boyd, Hazel and Heather
Thompson, Patricia King –
The lost girls in a ring
On a shadowy school playground
Like the nymphs dancing together
In the 'Allegory of Spring'.

FLIRTATION
&
COURTSHIP

ANONYMOUS (16th century)

She is My Dear *(from the Irish, translated by Frank O'Connor)*

She is my dear
Who makes me weep many a tear
And when I love far more of it
Than one that only brings good cheer

She is my own,
Day out day in she hears me groan,
And does not care if I am sad,
And would not grieve if I were gone.

She is my delight
She whose dear eyes are ever bright,
Whose hand will never prop my head,
Who will not turn to me at night.

She is my all
Who tells me nothing, great or small,
And does not see when I pass
And does not hear me when I call.

NAHUM TATE (1652-1715)

The Penance

Nymph fanaret, the gentlest maid
That ever happy swain obeyed,
(For what offense I cannot say)
A day and night, and half a day,
Banished her shepherd from her sight:
His fault for certain was not slight,
Or sure this tender judge had ne'er
Imposed a penance so severe.
And lest she should anon revoke
What in her warmer rage she spoke,
She bound the sentence with an oath,
Protested by her Faith and Troth,
Nought should compound for his offence
But the full time of abstinence.
Yet when his penance-glass were run,

His hours of castigation done,
Should he defer one moment's space
To come and be restored to grace,
With sparkling threat'ning eyes she swore
That failing would incense her more
Than all his trespasses before.

TURLOUGH O'CAROLAN (1670-1738)

Mabel Kelly *(from the Irish, translated by Austin Clarke)*

Lucky the husband
Who puts his hand beneath her head.
They kiss without scandal
Happiest two near feather-bed.
He sees the tumble of brown hair
Unplait, the breasts, pointed and bare
When nightdress shows
From dimple to toe-nail,
All Mabel glowing in it, here, there, everywhere.

Music might listen
To her least whisper,
Learn every note, for all are true.
While she is speaking,
Her voice goes sweetly
To charm the herons in their musing.
Her eyes are modest, blue, their darkness
Small rooms of thought, but when they sparkle
Upon a feast-day,
Glasses are meeting,
Each raised to Mabel Kelly, our toast and darling.

Gone now are many Irish ladies
Who kissed and fondled, their very pet-names
Forgotten, their tibia degraded.
She takes their sky. Her smile is famed.
Her praise is scored by quill and pencil.
Harp and spinet
Are in her debt
And when she plays or sings, melody is content.

No man who sees her
    Will feel uneasy.
He goes his way, head high, however tired.
    Lamp loses light
    When placed beside her.
She is the pearl and being of all Ireland
Foot, hand, eye, mouth, breast, thigh and instep, all that
    we desire.
Tresses that pass small curls as if to touch the ground;
    So many prizes
    Are not divided.
Her beauty is her own and she is not proud.

GEORGE FARQUHAR (1677-1707)

Thus Damon Knocked at Celia's Door

Thus Damon knocked at Celia's door,
Thus Damon knocked at Celia's door,
He sighed and begged and wept and swore,
The sign was so, she answered no,
The sign was so, she answered no, no, no no.

Again he sighed, again he prayed,
No, Damon, no, no, no, no, no, I am afraid;
Consider, Damon, I'm a maid,
Consider, Damon, no, no, no, no, no, no, I'm a Maid.

At last his sighs and tears made way,
She rose and softly turned the key;
Come in, said she, but do not, do not stay,
I may conclude, you will be rude;
But if you are you may:
I may conclude, you will be rude,
But if you are you may.

THOMAS PARNELL (1679-1718)

Song

My days have been so wondrous free,
 The little birds that fly
With careless ease from tree to tree,
 Were but as blest as I.

Ask gliding waters, if a tear
 Of mine increased their stream?
Or ask the flying gales, if e'er
 I lent one sigh to them?

But now my former days retire,
 And I'm by beauty caught,
The tender chains of sweet desire
 Are fixed upon my thought.

An eager hope within my breast
 Does every doubt control,
And charming Nancy stands confessed
 The favourite of my soul.

Ye nightingales, ye twisting pines,
 Ye swains that haunt the grove,
Ye gentle echoes, breezy winds,
 Ye close retreats of love –

With all of nature, all of art,
 Assist the dear design;
Oh, teach a young, unpractised heart
 To make her ever mine.

The very thought of change I hate,
 As much as of despair;
And hardly covet to be great,
 Unless it be for her.

'Tis true, the passion in my mind
 Is mixed with soft distress;
Yet while the fair I love is kind,
 I cannot wish it less.

SAMUEL SHEPHEARD (1701-1785)

To Miss Kitty Anym

You asked me what it was I said,
(and wonder I so soon forgot)
when my fond heart its thoughts betrayed
and sighed, and spoke, I know not what.

I'll swear the words I cannot tell
which foremost for their passage strove;
but this I can remember well,
that everything I said was love.

I counted not each word that flew,
but left my heart to guide my tongue;
and while I only thought of you,
I knew it could not lead me wrong.

How should I recollect the rest?
My heart was otherwise employed;
those lips, that bosom, when I pressed,
how could I think of aught beside?

You, if I erred, my errors made;
he, who, in forcing one dear kiss,
can stay to think of what he said,
shows he's unworthy of the bliss.

RICHARD BRINSLEY SHERIDAN (1751-1816)

I Ne'er Could Any Lustre See

I ne'er could any lustre see
In eyes that would not look on me;
I ne'er saw nectar on a lip,
But where my own did hope to sip.
Has the maid who seeks my heart
Cheeks of rose, untouched by art?
I will own the colour true,
When yielding blushes add their hue.

Is her hand so soft and pure?
I must press it, to be sure;
Nor can I be certain then,
Till it, grateful, press again.
Must I, with attentive eye,
Watch her heaving bosom sigh?
I will do so, when I see
That heaving bosom sigh for me.

THOMAS MOORE (1779-1852)

Mute Courtship *(from the Persian)*

Love hath a language of his own –
    A voice, that goes
From heart to heart – whose mystic tone
    Love only knows.

The lotus-flower, whose leaves I now
    Kiss silently,
Far more than words will tell thee how
    I worship thee.

The mirror, which to thee I hold –
    Which, when impressed
With thy bright looks, I turn and fold
    To this fond breast –

Doth it not speak, beyond all spells
    Of poet's art,
How deep thy hidden image dwells
    In this hushed heart?

SIR WILLIAM WILDE (1815-1876)

Les Lendemains *(after Dufresnay)*

Though Phyllis was fair, she was strangely capricious,
As she sat with her love 'neath the trees,
'In exchange you must give', said the maid avaricious
'Thirty sheep for one kiss, if you please!'

But the very next day things were vastly improving,
On our shepherd her gifts fortune rained –
For her, murmuring the tale of his passionate loving,
For one sheep thirty kisses obtained.

The third day she feared lest they might be denied her,
Those dainties for which her heart burned,
So raising her face to her lover beside her,
For one kiss all his sheep she returned.

Next day she'd have given up all she possessed
(When had pride such a terrible fall?)
Her sheep, dog, and crook, for the kiss the rogue pressed
On Lisette's lips for nothing at all!

AE [GEORGE RUSSELL] (1867-1935)

The Burning Glass

A shaft of fire that falls like dew,
    And melts and maddens all my blood,
From out thy spirit flashes through
    The burning-glass of womanhood.

Only so far; here must I stay:
    Nearer I miss the light, the fire;
I must endure the torturing ray,
    And with all beauty, all desire.

Ah, time long must the effort be,
    And far the way that I must go
To bring my spirit unto thee,
    Behind the glass, within the glow.

GEORGE ROBERTS (1873-1953)

Your Question

You ask me, sweetheart, to avow
    What charm in you I most adore,
But how can I discriminate
    From your innumerable store.

Yet 'tis not all you really are,
    Nor yet what I might wish to see,
But an ideal far above
    I worship – what you wish to be.

'Then pray,' you answer, 'tell me now
    What 'tis I most desire to be.'
Dear heart, your fondest dreams aspire
    To be – just what you are to me.

PADRAIC FALLON (1905-1975)

The River Walk

Disturbing it is
To take your stick sedately talking,
Evening in the water and the air;
And discover this: that a woman is a river.

The mythic properties are hard to bear.
Dismaying are
The ways she will intrude – if she intrude
Or merely assume the garments that you give her:
But a water willow stared at for so long
Glows graciously and knows the why you brood.

And such gesticulation –
Are you so young? – before the gentle birch
In its first shimmer: Lover, are you true
To one, or merely finding all you search
Brings the one woman home to you?

But how absurd to see
Her in that stilted bird, the heron in
A silt of river, all her blues pinned up:
In that brocaded goose the swan
For all her myths with Jupiter on top.

Dangerous, dangerous
This mythology. The doctors know it
And reason of it now like any poet.
Lover, go back no farther than your birth:
A woman is a woman, not the earth.

Her human business is
To resolve a man of other women always,
Not be, in a beautiful grotesque, all bodies
So various, a lover – if the girl insist
On love – must be a very pantheist.

NUALA NÍ DHOMHNAILL (b 1952)

Labasheedy (The Silken Bed)
(from the Irish, translated by the author)

I'd make a bed for you
in Labasheedy
in the tall grass
under the wrestling trees
where your skin
would be silk upon silk
in the darkness
when the moths are coming down.

Skin which glistens
shining over your limbs
like milk being poured
from jugs at dinnertime;
your hair is a herd of goats
moving over rolling hills,
hills that have high cliffs
and two ravines.

And your damp lips
would be as sweet as sugar
at evening and we walking
by the riverside
with honeyed breezes
blowing over the Shannon
and the fuchsias bowing down to you
one by one.

The fuchsias bending low
their solemn heads
in obeisance to the beauty
in front of them
I would pick a pair of flowers
as pendant earrings
to adorn you
like a bride in shining clothes.

O, I'd make a bed for you
in Labasheedy,
in the twilight hour
with evening falling slow
and what a pleasure it would be
to have our limbs entwine
wrestling
while the moths are coming down.

PRAISE
&
DEVOTION

ANONYMOUS (16th-18th century)

Aileen Aroon (*from the Irish, translated by Gerald Griffin*)

When, like the early rose,
  Aileen aroon!
Beauty in childhood blows,
  Aileen aroon!
When, like a diadem,
Buds blush around the stem,
Which is the fairest gem?
  Aileen aroon!

Is it the laughing eye?
  Aileen aroon!
Is it the timid sigh?
  Aileen aroon!
Is it the tender tone,
Soft as the stringed harp's moan?
Oh, it is truth alone,
  Aileen aroon!

When, like the rising day,
  Aileen aroon!
Love sends his early ray,
  Aileen aroon!
What makes his dawning glow
Changeless through joy or woe?
Only the constant know,
  Aileen aroon!

I knew a valley fair,
  Aileen aroon!
I knew a cottage there,
  Aileen aroon!
Far in the valley's shade
I knew a gentle maid,
Flower of the hazel glade,
  Aileen aroon!

Who in the song so sweet,
    Aileen aroon!
Who in the dance so sweet,
    Aileen aroon!
Dear were her charms to me,
Dearer her laughter free,
Dearest her constancy,
    Aileen aroon!

Were she no longer true,
    Aileen aroon!
What should her lover do?
    Aileen aroon!
Fly with his broken chain
Far o'er the sounding main,
Never to love again,
    Aileen aroon!

Youth must with time decay,
    Aileen aroon!
Beauty must fade away,
    Aileen aroon!
Castles are sacked in war,
Chieftains are scattered far,
Truth is a fixed star,
    Aileen aroon!

ANONYMOUS (17th-19th century)

Brídín Vesey *(from the Irish, translated by Donagh MacDonagh)*

I would marry Brídín Vesey
Without a shoe or petticoat,
A comb, a cloak or dowry
Or even one clean shift;
And I would make novena
Or imitate the hermits
Who spend their lives in fasting
All for a Christmas gift.
O cheek like dogwood fruiting,
O cuckoo of the mountain,

I would send darkness packing
If you would rise and go
Against the ban of clergy
And the sour lips of your parents
And take me at an altar-stone
In spite of all Mayo.

That was the sullen morning
They told the cruel story,
How scorning word or token
You rose and went away.
'Twas then my hands remembered,
My ears still heard you calling,
I smelt the gorse and heather
Where you first learned to pray.
What could they know, who named you,
Of jug and bed and table,
Hours slipping through our fingers,
Time banished from the room?
Or what of all the secrets
We knew among the rushes
Under the Reek when cuckoos
Brightened against the moon?

You are my first and last song,
The harp that lilts my fingers
Your lips like frozen honey,
Eyes like the mountain pool,
Shaped like the Reek your breast is,
Whiter than milk from Nephin,
And he who never saw you
Has lived and died a fool.
Oh, gone across the mearing
Dividing hope from sadness
What happy townland holds you?
In what country do you reign?
In spite of all the grinning lads
At corner and in haybarn,
I'll search all Ireland over
And bring you home again.

ANONYMOUS (17th century)

Cashel of Munster (from the Irish, translated by Edward Walsh)

I would wed you, dear, without gold or gear, or counted kine,
My wealth you'll be, would fair friends agree, and you be mine.
My grief, my gloom! That you do not come, my heart's dear hoard!
To Cashel fair, though our couch were there, but a hard deal board.

O come, my bride, o'er the wild hill-side to the valley low!
A downy bed for my love I'll spread, where waters flow,
And we shall stray where streamlets play, the groves among,
Where echo tells to the listening dells the blackbird's song.
Love tender, true, I gave to you, and secret sighs,
In hope to see upon you and me one hour arise,
When the priest's blest voice would bind my choice and the
      ring's shirt tie,
If wife you be, love, to one but me, love, in grief I'll die.

A neck of white has my heart's delight, and breast like snow,
And flowing hair whose ringlets fair to the green grass flow,
Alas, that I do not early die, before the day
That saw me here, from my bosom's dear, far, far away.

ANONYMOUS (17th-18th century)

She (from the Irish, translated by Eleanor Hull)

The white bloom of the blackthorn, she,
      The small sweet raspberry-blossom, she;
More fair the shy, rare glance of her eye,
      Than the wealth of the world to me.

My heart's pulse, my secret, she,
      The flower of the fragrant apple, she;
A summer glow o'er the winter's snow,
      'Twixt Christmas and Easter, she.

ANONYMOUS (17th-18th century)

The Snowy-Breasted Pearl
(from the Irish, translated by Sir George Petrie)

There's a colleen fair as May,
For a year and for a day
I've sought by every way her heart to gain.
There's no art of tongue or eye
Fond youths with maidens try
But I've tried with ceaseless sigh, yet tried in vain.
If to France or far-off Spain
She'd cross the watery main,
To see her face again the sea I'd brave.
And if 'tis heaven's decree
That mine she may not be
May the son of Mary me in mercy save!

O thou blooming milk-white dove,
To whom I've given true love,
Do not ever thus reprove my constancy.
There are maidens would be mine,
With wealth in hand and kine,
If my heart would but incline to turn from thee.
But a kiss with welcome bland,
And a touch of thy dear hand,
Are all that I demand, would'st thou not spurn;
For if not mine, dear girl,
O Snowy-Breasted Pearl!
May I never from the fair with life return!

THOMAS 'LAIDIR' COSTELLO (mid-17th century)

Úna Bhán *(from the Irish, translated by Thomas Kinsella)*

Úna fair, my flower of the amber tresses,
who have found your death on account of evil counsel,
see now, my caged love, which of the two counsels
was the better, and I in a ford in the Donogue river.

Úna fair, you have left me knotted in sorrow,
but what use talking about it again for ever?
Ringleted locks with the melted gold ascending,
I would rather be near you than all the glory of Heaven.

Úna fair, it was you that upset my senses.
Úna, you came between me and my God, and deeply.
Úna, my fragrant branch, little coiling curl,
I'd better have been without eyes than ever have seen you.

A piercing pain: young Úna nic Dhiarmada!
Fragrant branch, sweet-mannered, with speech like music;
sugar-sweet mouth, milk-fresh, like ale or wine;
foot supple of step and easy inside a shoe.

Úna, my heart, my limb, of the soft fresh breasts,
tempting green eyes, fine hair flowing yellow and thick,
let your dowry be a hundred cows – five hundred horses! –
I would choose yourself above all you might bring of treasure.

I had travelled and hard the journey, through every province,
but her parents refused my hand though fine and open.
The choicest flower of the Búille, and generous with cattle,
what good was it guarding her from me and letting her perish?

Úna fair, like a rose you were in a garden
or a candlestick of gold on a queenly table.
You were song and music upon the way before me.
Ruin – bitter dawn: you not wed to your dark beloved.

PIERCE FERRITER (d 1653)

Lay Your Arms Aside (from the Irish, translated by Eiléan ní Chuilleanáin)

Gentlest of women, put your weapons by,
Unless you want to ruin all mankind;
Leave the assault or I must make reply,
Proclaiming that you are murderously inclined.
Put by your armour, lay your darts to rest,
Hide your soft hair and all its devious ways:
To see it lie in coils upon your breast
Poisons all hope and mercilessly slays.

Protest you never murdered in your life;
You lie: your hand's smooth touch, your well-shaped knee
Destroy as easily as axe or knife.
Your breasts like new spring flowers, your naked side
– I cry for aid to heaven – conceal from me;
Let shame for the destruction you have made
Hide your bright eyes, your shining teeth, away;
If all our sighs and trembling and dismay
Can touch your heart or satisfy your pride,
Gentlest of women, lay your arms aside.

JONATHAN SWIFT (1667-1745)

Lines from Cadenus to Vanessa

Nymph, would you learn the only art
To keep a worthy lover's heart?
First, to adorn your person well,
In utmost cleanliness excel,
And though you must the fashions take,
Observe them but for fashion's sake.

The strongest reason will submit
To virtue, honour, sense, and wit.
To such a nymph the wise and good
Cannot be faithless if they would:
For vices all have different ends,
But virtue still to virtue tends.
And when your lover is not true,
'Tis virtue fails in him or you:
And either he deserves disdain,
Or you without a cause complain.
But here Vanessa cannot err,
Nor are these rules applied to her:
For who could such a nymph forsake
Except a blockhead or a rake,
Or how could she her heart bestow
Except where wit and virtue grow.

JONATHAN SWIFT

Stella's Birthday

This day whate'er the Fates decree,
Shall still be kept with joy by me:
This day then let us not be told
That you are sick, and I grown old,
Nor think on our approaching ills,
And talk of spectacles and pills;
Tomorrow will be time enough
To hear such mortifying stuff.
Yet since from reason may be brought
A better and more pleasing thought,
Which can, in spite of all decays,
Support a few remaining days;
From not the gravest of divines
Accept for once some serious lines.

Although we now can form no more
Long schemes of life as heretofore;
Yet you, while time is running fast
Can look with joy on what is past.

Were future happiness and pain,
A mere contrivance of the brain,
As atheists argue, to entice
And fit their proselytes for vice;
(The only comfort they propose,
To have companions in their woes).
Grant this the case, yet sure 'tis hard
That virtue styled its own reward,
And by all sages understood
To be the chief of human good,
Should acting, die, nor leave behind
Some lasting pleasure in the mind,
Which by remembrance will assuage
Grief, sickness, poverty and age;
And strongly shoot a radiant dart
To shine through life's declining part.

Say, *Stella*, feel you no content
Reflecting on a life well spent?
Your skilful hand employed to save
Despairing wretches from the grave;
And then supporting with your store
Those whom you dragged from death before
(So Providence on mortals waits,
Preserving what it just creates)
Your generous boldness to defend
An innocent and absent friend;
That courage which can make you just
To merit humbled in the dust:
The detestation you express
For vice in all its glittering dress:
That patience under torturing pain,
Where stubborn stoics would complain.

Shall these like empty shadows pass,
Or forms reflected from a glass?
Or mere chimeras in the mind,
That fly and leave no marks behind?
Does not the body thrive and grow
By food of twenty years ago?
And, had it not been still supplied
It must a thousand times have died:
Then, who with reason can maintain
That no effects of food remain?
And is not virtue in mankind
The nutriment that feeds the mind?
Upheld by each good action past,
And still continued by the last:
Then, who with reason can pretend
That all effects of virtue end?

Believe me *Stella*, when you show
That true contempt for things below,
Nor prize your life for other ends
Than merely to oblige your friends;
Your former actions claim their part,
And join to fortify your heart.

For virtue in her daily race,
Like Janus, bears a double face;
Looks back with joy where she has gone,
And therefore goes with courage on.
She at your sickly couch will wait,
And guide you to a better state.

O then, whatever Heaven intends,
Take pity on your pitying friends;
Nor let your ills affect your mind,
To fancy they can be unkind.
Me, surely me, you ought to spare,
Who gladly would your sufferings share;
Or give my scrap of life to you,
And think it far beneath your due,
You, to whose care so oft I owe,
That I'm alive to tell you so.

ESTHER VAN HOMRIGH ['VANESSA'] (1688-1723)
Hail, Blushing Goddess, Beauteous Spring

Hail, blushing goddess, beauteous Spring!
Who, in thy jocund train dost bring
Loves and graces, smiling hours,
Balmy breezes, fragrant flowers;
Come, with tints of roseate hue,
Nature's faded charms renew.
      Yet why should I thy presence hail?
To me no more the breathing gale
Comes fraught with sweets, no more the rose
With such transcendent beauty blows,
As when Cadenus blest the scene,
And shared with me those joys serene.
When, unperceived, the lambent fire
Of friendship kindled new desire;
Still listening to his tuneful tongue,

41

The truths which angels might have sung
Divine impressed, their gentle sway,
And sweetly stole my soul away.
    My guide, instructor, lover, friend,
Dear names in one idea blend;
Oh! still conjoined, your incense rise,
And waft sweet odours to the skies.

ANONYMOUS (?18th century)

The Girl I Love (from the Irish, translated by J. J. Callanan)

The girl I love is comely, straight and tall;
Down her white neck her auburn tresses fall;
Her dress is neat, her carriage light and free –
Here's a health to that charming maid, whoe'er she be!

The rose's blush but fades beside her cheek;
Her eyes are blue, her forehead pale and meek;
Her lips are cherries on a summer tree –
Here's a health to the charming maid, whoe'er she be!

When I go to the field no youth can lighter bound,
And I freely pay when the cheerful jug goes round;
The barrel is full; but its heart we soon shall see –
Come, here's to that charming maid, who'er she be!

Had I the wealth that props the Saxon's reign,
Or the diamond crown that decks the King of Spain,
I'd yield them all if she kindly smiled on me –
Here's a health to the maid I love, who'er she be!

Five pounds of gold for each lock of her hair I'd pay,
And five times five, for my love one hour each day;
Her voice is more sweet than the thrush on its own green tree –
Then, my dear, may I drink a fond deep health to thee!

ANONYMOUS (?18th-19th century)
My Love is Like a Cabbage *(Oral poem from Tyrone)*

My love is like a cabbage
    That's easy cut in two.
The leaves I'll give to others
    But the heart I'll keep for you.

ANONYMOUS (18th century)
On Deborah Perkins of the County of Wicklow

Some sing ye of Venus the goddess
Some chant ye of rills, and of fountains;
    But the theme of such praise,
    As my fancy can raise,
Is a wench of the Wicklow mountains.

Mount Ida they surely surpass,
With the Wood-nymphs recess, and their lurkings;
    O! 'tis there that I play
    And wanton all day,
With little black Deborah Perkins.

King Solomon, he had nine hundred, at least,
To humour his taste, with their smirkings;
    But not one of 'em all,
    When she led up a ball,
Could foot it like Deborah Perkins.

The fair Cleopatra, Anthony loved,
But, by heaven, I'd give him his jerkings;
    If that he was here,
    And shou'd think to compare
That trollop, with Deborah Perkins.

Bacchus he prized Ariadne the sweet,
But I wish we were now at the firkins;
    I'd make him reel off,
    In contemptible scoff,
While I toasted plump Deborah Perkins.

Might I have all the girls at command,
That boast of their Dresden, or markings;
I'd rather feed goats,
And play with the coats
Of cherry-cheeked Deborah Perkins.

A fig for the eclogues of Maro,
Or Ovid's fantastical workings;
If I haven't their letters,
I sing of their betters,
When I touch up young Deborah Perkins.

ANONYMOUS (?18th century)

Pulse of My Heart (*from the Irish, translated by Charlotte Brooke*)

As the sweet blackberry's modest bloom,
Fair flowering, greets the sight,
Or strawberries, in their rich perfume,
Fragrance and bloom unite:
So this fair plant of tender youth
In outward charms can vie,
And from within the soul of truth,
Soft beaming fills her eye.
Pulse of my heart! Dear source of care,
Stolen sighs, and love-breathed vows!
Sweeter than when through scented air
Gay bloom the apple boughs!
With thee no day can winter seem,
Nor frost nor blast can chill;
Thou the soft breeze, the cheering team,
That keeps it summer still.

JAMES EYRE WEEKES (?1719-?1754)

To a Lady with a Fan

Go, cooling fan, and let my Anna see
how near thy form her eyes have rendered me,
a mere anatomy! Thy ribs like mine
with nothing on them but a painted skin.

Go, cooling fan, import thy cooling breeze
to those white regions which already freeze,
those icy breasts, where snow eternal lies,
nor melts, though near the sunshine of her eyes.

Go, cooling fan, and in thy folds enclose
those sultry sighs with which my body glows,
go tell the fair one that the love-sick boy
is like the messenger he sends, her toy,
flirted and twirled and furled and twirled again,
like sails obedient to the winds and rain.

Say that her presence, as the sun the rose,
spreads all my hopes and all my blushes shows,
say, when she's gone, my folding hopes decay,
are furled like thee and wait her hand to play.

JOHN O'KEEFE (1747-1833)

Amo, Amas

Amo, Amas, I love a lass
As a cedar tall and slender;
Sweet cowslip's grace is her nominative case,
And she's of the feminine gender.

Rorum, Corum, sunt divorum,
Harum, Scarum divo;
Tag-rag, merry-derry, periwig and hat-band
Hic hoc horum genitivo.

Can I decline a Nymph divine?
Her voice as a flute is dulcis.
Her oculus bright, her manus white,
And soft, when I tacto, her pulse is.

>Rorum, Corum, sunt divorum,
>Harum, Scarum divo;
>Tag-rag, merry-derry, periwig and hat-band
>Hic hoc horum genitivo.

Oh, how bella my puella,
I'll kiss secula seculorum.
If I've luck, sir, she's my uxor,
O dies benedictorum.

>Rorum, Corum, sunt divorum,
>Harum, Scarum divo;
>Tag-rag, merry-derry, periwig and hat-band
>Hic hoc horum genitivo.

RICHARD BRINSLEY SHERIDAN (1751-1816)

Dry Be That Tear

>Dry be that tear, my gentlest love,
>   Be hushed that struggling sigh;
>Nor seasons, day, nor fate shall prove
>   More fixed, more true than I.
>Hushed be that sigh, be dry that tear,
>Cease boding doubt, cease anxious fear,
>   Dry be that tear.

>Ask'st thou how long my love will stay,
>   When all that's new is past?
>How long, ah Delia! can I say
>   How long my life will last?
>Dry be that tear, be hushed that sigh,
>At least I'll love thee till I die.
>   Hushed be that sigh.

And does that thought affect thee too,
    The thought of Sylvio's death,
That he who only breathed for you
    Must yield that faithful breath?
Hushed be that sigh, be dry that tear,
Nor let us lose our heaven here.
    Dry be that tear.

JAMES CLARENCE MANGAN (1803-1849)

Dark Rosaleen

O my dark Rosaleen,
    Do no sigh, do not weep!
The priests are on the ocean green,
    They march along the deep.
There's wine from the royal Pope,
    Upon the ocean green;
And Spanish ale shall give you hope,
    My dark Rosaleen!
    My own Rosaleen!
Shall glad your heart, shall give you hope,
Shall give you health and help, and hope,
    My dark Rosaleen.

Over hills, and through dales,
    Have I roamed for your sake;
All yesterday I sailed with sails
    On river and on lake.
The Erne, at its highest flood,
    I dashed across unseen,
For there was lightning in my blood,
    My dark Rosaleen!
    My own Rosaleen!
Oh! there was lightning in my blood,
Red lightning, lightened through my blood,
    My dark Rosaleen!

All day long in unrest,
    To and fro do I move,
The very soul within my breast
    Is wasted for you, love!
The heart in my bosom faints
    To think of you, my Queen,
My life of life, my saint of saints,
    My dark Rosaleen!
    My own Rosaleen!
To hear your sweet and sad complaints,
My life, my love, my saint of saints,
    My dark Rosaleen!

Woe and pain, pain and woe,
    Are my lot, night and noon,
To see your bright face clouded so,
    Like to the mournful moon.
But yet will I rear your throne
    Again in golden sheen;
'Tis you shall reign, shall reign alone,
    My dark Rosaleen!
    My own Rosaleen!
'Tis you shall have the golden throne,
'Tis you shall reign, shall reign alone,
    My dark Rosaleen!

Over dews, over sands,
    Will I fly for your weal:
Your holy, delicate white hands
    Shall girdle me with steel.
At home in your emerald bowers,
    From morning's dawn to e'en,
You'll pray for me, my flower of flowers,
    My dark Rosaleen!
    My fond Rosaleen!
You'll think of me your daylight's hours,
My virgin flower, my flower of flowers,
    My dark Rosaleen!

I could scale the blue air,
　　I could plough the high hills,
Oh, I could kneel all night in prayer,
　　To heal your many ills!
And one beamy smile from you
　　Would float like light between
My toils and me, my own, my true,
　　My dark Rosaleen!
　　My fond Rosaleen!
Would give me life and soul anew,
A second life, a soul anew,
　　My dark Rosaleen!

O! the Erne shall run red
　　With redundance of blood,
The earth shall rock beneath our tread,
　　And flames wrap hill and wood,
And gun-peal, and slogan cry
　　Wake many a glen serene,
'Ere you shall fade, 'ere you shall die,
　　My dark Rosaleen!
　　My own Rosaleen!
The Judgement Hour must first be nigh
'Ere you can fade, 'ere you can die,
　　My dark Rosaleen!

SIR SAMUEL FERGUSON (1810-1886)

The Lark in the Clear Air

Dear thoughts are in my mind
And my soul soars enchanted,
As I hear the sweet lark sing
In the clear air of the day.
For a tender beaming smile
To my hope has been granted,
And tomorrow she shall hear
All my fond heart would say.

I shall tell her all my love,
All my soul's adoration;
And I think she will hear me
And will not say me nay.
It is this that fills my soul
With its joyous elation,
As I hear the sweet lark sing
In the clear air of the day.

JOHN BOYLE O'REILLY (1844-1890)

A White Rose

The red rose whispers of passion,
    And the white rose breathes of love;
O, the red rose is a falcon,
    And the white rose is a dove.

But I send you a cream-white rosebud
    With a flush on its petal tips;
For the love that is purest and sweetest
    Has a kiss of desire on the lips.

G. F. SAVAGE ARMSTRONG (1845-1906)

The Yin Wee Luiv

As at the boord apart she sat,
An' noo tae this yin noo tae that
She talked wi' careless kin'ness,
Fu' weel A kenned her inmaist heart
In a' she said had little pert,
Uv hai'f the words she heerd wuz min'less.
An' though she seemed tae shun my sight,
A trusted mair her luve that night
Than a' Airth's luves thegither;
Then yin wee gentle luik she gave.
A'd waited lang that luik tae haive
An' lay A'd want fur sich anither.

WILLIAM BUTLER YEATS (1865-1939)

He Wishes for the Cloths of Heaven

> Had I the heavens' embroidered cloths,
> Enwrought with golden and silver light,
> The blue and the dim and the dark cloths
> Of night and light and the half-light,
> I would spread the cloths under your feet:
> But I, being poor, have only my dreams;
> I have spread my dreams under your feet;
> Tread softly because you tread on my dreams.

JOHN MILLINGTON SYNGE (1871-1909)

Queens

> Seven dog-days we let pass
> Naming Queens in Glenmacnass,
> All the rare and royal names
> Wormy sheepskin yet retains,
> Etain, Helen, Maeve, and Fand,
> Golden Deirdre's tender hand,
> Bert, the big-foot, sung by Villon,
> Cassandra, Ronsard found in Lyon.
> Queens of Sheba, Meath and Connaught,
> Coifed with crown, or gaudy bonnet,
> Queens whose finger once did stir men,
> Queens were eaten of fleas and vermin,
> Queens men drew like Monna Lisa,
> Or slew with drugs in Rome and Pisa,
> We named Lucrezia Crivelli,
> And Titian's lady with amber belly,
> Queens acquainted in learned sin,
> Jane of Jewry's slender shin:
> Queens who cut the bogs of Glanna,
> Judith of Scripture, and Gloriana,
> Queens who wasted the East by proxy,
> Or drove the ass-cart, a tinker's doxy,
> Yet these are rotten – I ask their pardon –
> And we've the sun on rock and garden,
> These are rotten, so you're the Queen
> Of all are living, or have been.

SEUMAS O'SULLIVAN (1879-1958)

The Grey Dusk

I

Tremulous grey of dusk,
    Deepening into the blue,
It is the path that leads
    Ever to you.

Child of the dusk, your eyes
    Quietly light my way,
Quiet as evening stars,
    Quiet and grey.

All the magic of dusk,
    Tremulous, grey and blue,
Gathers into my heart,
    Quiet for you.

II

Child, I thought that we two by some grey sea
    Went walking very quietly, hand in hand,
    By a grey sea along a silent strand,
And you had turned your eyes away from me
To where grey clouds, uplifted mightily,
    Made on the far horizon a silver land,
And I would not recall your eyes to me,
    Because I knew from your shy clasping hand
How joy within your heart, a wanderer long,
    Outwearied now had come, a nesting bird,
And folded there his wings, too glad for song;
    And so I knew at last that you had heard
Through the long miles of grey sea-folding mist,
    Soft as the breast of some glad nesting dove,
From grey lips grown articulate, twilight-kissed,
    All the secret of my unuttered love.

FRANCIS LEDWIDGE (1887-1917)

Had I a Golden Pound *(after the Irish)*

Had I a golden pound to spend,
My love should mend and sew no more.
And I would buy her a little quern,
Easy to turn at the kitchen floor

And for her wondrous curtains white,
With birds in flight and flowers in bloom,
To face with pride the road to town,
And mellow down her sunlit room

And with the silver change we'd prove
The truth of Love to life's own end,
With hearts the year could but embolden,
Had I a golden pound to spend.

F. R. HIGGINS (1896-1941)

O You Among Women

When pails empty the last brightness
Of the well, at twilight-time
And you are there among women –
O mouth of silence,
Will you come with me, when I sign,
To the fair green wood, that fences
A lake inlaid with light?

To be there, O, lost in each other,
While day melts in airy water,
And the drake-headed pike – a shade
In the waves' pale stir!
For love is there, under the breath,
As a coy star is there in the quiet
Of the wood's blue eye.

PATRICK MacDONOGH (1902-1961)

Be Still as You are Beautiful

Be still as you are beautiful,
    Be silent as the rose;
Through miles of starlit countryside
    Unspoken worship flows
To find you in your loveless room
    From lonely men whom daylight gave
The blessing of your passing face
    Impenetrably grave.

A white owl in the lichened wood
    Is circling silently,
More secret and more silent yet
    Must be your love to me.
Thus, while about my dreaming head
    Your soul in ceaseless vigil goes,
Be still as you are beautiful,
    Be silent as the rose.

CECIL DAY-LEWIS (1904-1959)
Now She is Like the White Tree-Rose

Now she is like the white tree-rose
That takes a blessing from the sun:
Summer has filled her veins with light,
And her warm heart is washed with noon.

Or as a poplar, ceaselessly
Gives a soft answer to the wind:
Cool on the light her leaves lie sleeping,
Folding a column of sweet sound.

Powder the stars. Forbid the night
To wear those brilliants for a brooch
So soon, dark death, you may close down
The mines that made this beauty rich.

Her thoughts are pleiads, stooping low
O'er glades where nightingale has flown:
And like the luminous night around her
She has at heart a certain dawn.

SAMUEL BECKETT (1906-1989)
I Would Like My Love to Die
(from the French, translated by the author)

I would like my love to die
and the rain to be falling on the graveyard
and on me walking the streets
mourning the first and last to love me.

ROBERT FARREN (1909-1984)

No Woman Born

Young head in sunlight! Not a woman born
has lifted head like her head; plenty's horn
poured no alight abundance like her hair.
Wonder is on her lids like the bright air.
She wakes to worship, and draws on dull mouths to prayer.
There is, to be named one with her, no woman born.

EITHNE STRONG (b 1923)

Dedication

To you
I have given.
I want to be with you
along the way you have chosen.
To work
to flow the vital current of my life
towards our high vision.
To be about you
holding your being that I have not yet touched
near to the untouched hiddenness of me.
I need the wonder of you
that I have known
on magnificent mornings
to be fresh upon me;
and the smell of summer
to be in my blood;
and the lark-song that we have heard
on dry hot days on mountains
to beat in me
forever.

CAITLÍN MAUDE (1941-1982)

Entreaty *(from the Irish, translated by Gabriel Fitzmaurice)*

Young man,
do not come near me,
do not speak ...
the words of love
are sweet –
but sweeter still
is the word
that was never uttered –
no choice
is without stain –
the choice of words
is much the same
and this would be
to choose between evils
in our present
situation ...

Do not break
the clear glass
between us
      (no glass is broken
      without blood and pain)
for beyond is
Heaven
or beyond is Hell
and what good is
Heaven
if it is not
for ever? –
the loss of
Heaven
is the worst Hell ...

I again implore you,
do not speak,
young man,
my 'Diarmaid',
and we will be at peace –
untouchable understanding
between us
we will have no cause
to touch it
ever
as it ever
alures us –
but I implore you ...
do not speak ...

DERMOT BOLGER (b 1959)

Stardust

Last night in swirling colour we danced again
and as strobe lights stunned in black and white
I reached in this agony of slow motion for you
but you danced on as if cold light still shone
merging into the crown as my path was blocked
by snarling bouncers and the dead-eyed club owner

when I screamed across the music nobody heard
I flailed under spotlights like a disco dancer
and they formed a circle clapping to the beat
as I shuddered round the club in a violent fit
hurling through a dream without trembling awake
I revolved through space until I hit the ground

Lying among their feet tramping out the tunes
I grasped you inside my mind for this moment
your white dress bobbing in a cool candleflame
illuminating the darkness spinning towards me
a teenage dancing queen proud of her footwork
sparks rising like stardust all over the floor.

ENCOUNTERS

ANONYMOUS (?18th-19th century)

Youghal Harbour

(from the Irish, translated by Sir Samuel Ferguson)

One Sunday morning, into Youghal walking,
    I met a maiden upon the way;
Her little mouth sweet as fairy music,
    Her soft cheek blushing like dawn of day!
I laid a bold hand upon her bosom,
    And asked a kiss: but she answered: 'No:
Fair sir, be gentle; do not tear my mantle;
    'Tis none in Erin my grief can know.

'Tis but a little hour since I left Youghal,
    And my love forbade me to return;
And now my weary way I wander
    Into Cappoquin, a poor girl forlorn:
Then do not tempt me; for, alas, I dread them
    Who with tempting proffers teach girls to roam
Who'd first deceive us, then faithless leave us,
    And send us shame-faced and bare-foot home.'

'My heart and hand here! I mean you marriage!
    I have loved like you and known love's pain;
And if you turn back now to Youghal Harbour,
    You ne'er shall want house or home again:
You shall have a lace cap like any lady,
    Cloak and capuchin, too, to keep you warm,
And if God pleases, maybe, a little baby,
    By and by, to nestle within your arm.'

ANTOINE Ó RAIFTERAÍ (1784-1835)

Mary Hynes of Baile-laoi (*from the Irish, translated by Lady Gregory*)

Going to Mass, by the will of God
The day came wet and the wind rose;
I met Mary Hynes at the cross of Kiltartan
And I fell in love with her then and there.

I spoke to her kind and mannerly
As by report was her own way;
And she said, 'Raftery, my mind is easy,
You may come to-day to Baile-laoi.'

When I heard her offer I did not linger,
When her talk went to my heart my heart rose.
We had only to go across the three fields,
We had daylight with us to Baile-laoi.

The table was laid with glasses and a quart measure;
She had fair hair and she sitting beside me,
And she said 'Drink, Raftery, and a hundred welcomes,
There is a strong cellar in Baile-laoi.'

O star of light, and O sun in harvest,
O amber hair, O my share of the world,
Will you come with me upon Sunday
Till we agree together before all the people?

I would not grudge you a song every Sunday evening,
Punch on the table or wine if you would drink it,
But, O King of Glory, dry the roads before me,
Till I find the way to Baile-laoi.

There is sweet air on the side of the hill
When you are looking down upon Baile-laoi;
When you are walking in the valley picking nuts and blackberries
There is music of the birds in it and music of the sidhe.

What is the worth of greatness till you have the light
Of the flower of the branch that is by your side?
There is no good to deny it or to try to hide it,
She is the sun in the heavens who wounded my heart.

There is no part of Ireland I did not travel
From the rivers to the tops of the mountains,
To the edge of Loch Greine whose mouth is hidden,
And I saw no beauty but was behind hers.

Her hair was shining and her brows were shining, too;
Her face was like herself, her mouth pleasant and sweet;
She is my pride, and I give her the branch,
She is the shining flower of Baile-laoi.

It is Mary Hynes, the calm and easy woman,
Her beauty in her mind and in her face.
If a hundred clerks were gathered together,
They could not write down a half of her ways.

JAMES CLARENCE MANGAN (1803-1849)

And Then No More

I saw her once, one little while, and then no more:
'Twas Eden's light on Earth awhile, and then no more.
Amid the throng she passed along the meadow-floor:
Spring seemed to smile on Earth awhile, and then no more;
But whence she came, which way she went, what garb she
    wore
I noted not; I gazed awhile, and then no more!

I saw her once, one little while, and then no more!
'Twas Paradise on Earth awhile, and then no more.
Ah! what avail my vigils pale, my magic lore?
She shone before mine eyes awhile, and then no more.
The shallop of my peace is wrecked on Beauty's shore.
Near Hope's fair isle it rode awhile, and then no more!

I saw her once, one little while, and then no more:
Earth looked like Heaven a little while, and then no more.
Her presence thrilled and lighted to its inner core
My desert breast a little while, and then no more.
So may, perchance, a meteor glance at midnight o'er
Some ruined pile a little while, and then no more!

I saw her once, one little while, and then no more:
The earth was Peri-land awhile, and then no more.
Oh, might I see but once again, as once before,
Through chance or wile, that shape awhile,
     and then no more!
Death soon would heal my griefs! This heart,
     now sad and sore,
Would beat anew a little while, and then no more.

MONK GIBBON (1896-1987)

Song

Singer within the little streets,
Sing her a song about a fool who came,
Looked in her eyes, and in that moment knew
Nothing would be the same.

Ever again, a fool who hardly knew
When the stars shone, or when the slanting rain,
Beat on his face, or anything at all
Or any pain

Save the one pain – tomorrow might not come,
Or any fear – save that he should be blind,
Or any thought – save that her words were sweet
Her eyes were kind.

RHODA COGHILL (b 1903)
Poem

Is to love this – to nurse a name,
The symbol of a person, of a presence,
As when a novice invokes her saint,
And the sweet title's murmured once every second?

And is it to create, merging the false and true,
A not-impossible world of miracle,
Where intuition strains to know the absolute,
And fantasy seems more certain than things visible?

More than this. Lover and mystic, stirred, spirit-shaken,
Yield to an instant urge, shape the will newly,
Take the shock, unresisting, of storm and danger,
Accept the implications of a curve, subdued to
    the wave's beauty.

W. R. RODGERS (1909-1969)
Stormy Night

Is this the street? Never a sign of life,
The swinging lamp throws everything about;
But see! from that sly doorway, like a knife
The gilt edge of inviting light slides out
And in again – the very sign
Of her whose slightest nod I lately thought was mine;

But not now.
Knock! and the night-flowering lady
Opens, and across the brilliant sill
Sees me standing there so dark and shady
Hugging the silences of my ill-will;
Wildly she turns from me – but no, my love,
This foot's within the door, this hand's without the glove.

Well may you tremble now, and say there was nothing meant,
And curl away from my care with a 'Please, my dear!',
For though you were smoke, sucked up by a raging vent,
I'd follow you through every flue of your fear,
And over your faraway arms I'll mountain and cone
In a pillar of carolling fire and fountaining stone.

O strike the gong of your wrong, raise the roof of your rage
Fist and foist me off with a cloud of cries,
What do I care for all your footling rampage?
On your light-in-gale blows my larking caresses will rise,
But – Why so still? What? are you weeping, my sweet?
Ah heart, heart, look! I throw myself at your feet.

DONAGH MacDONAGH (1912-1968)

Going to Mass Last Sunday (Tune: The Lowlands of Holland)

Going to Mass last Sunday my true love passed me by,
I knew her mind was altered by the rolling of her eye;
And when I stood in God's dark light my tongue could
    word no prayer
Knowing my saint had fled and left her reliquary bare.

Sweet faces smiled from holy glass, demure in saintly love,
Sweet voices ripe with Latin grace rolled from the choir above;
But brown eyes under Sunday wear were all my liturgy;
How can she hope for heaven who has so deluded me?

When daffodils were altar gold her lips were light on mine
And when the hawthorn flame was bright we drank the
    year's new wine;
The nights seemed stained-glass windows lit with love
    that paled the sky,
But love's last ember perishes in the winter of her eye.

Drape every downcast day now in purple cloth of Lent,
Smudge every forehead now with ash, that she may yet repent,
Who going to Mass last Sunday could pass so proudly by
And show her mind was altered by the rolling of an eye.

EUGENE WATTERS (1919-1984)

from The Week-End of Dermot and Grace

... She beckoned and smiled when eyes met,
The dark girl welcoming me;
The tired air of the thirdclass compartment
Smelled of Aphrodité;
The man with frayed collarband and friendly eyes
Spat delicately;
The linked train took us into the afternoon
As from under the yews of a churchyard calvary.

Let us alone, man of the friendly eyes
And big, brass honest collarstud;
We have stolen no fire from heaven, none from hell,
We were not with Agamemnon outside Troy
Nor above the Japanese town whose name
Is a phrase of the mating thrush's eastersong.
Why trouble us? We have no ambition
To nail any man to a timber cross
For claiming he was Gandhi born again,
Born greater. What have we to do with you?

... Thrum of the contrived wheel turning.
Let us alone. The bright day is free.
We talked thinly of the meeting at Strasburg,
The paper at one page was full of it,
Epical headline and flash photograph
Of men's fine fingers that are never easy.
Let us alone. The bright day is free.
May be our only hope, I said yawning,
When I was in England, she said brightening,
Listen to me now, the quiet man said
Burdening us both in turn with the friendliness of his eyes
And with one brown workman's hand
Covering her knee –
Alone, alone, old man, the bright day is free.
I have not borne her out of Sparta,
I am no two-o'clock Tarquin,

No Pluto with a motorcar in a dark lane.
We two have sheltered under the one umbrella
While the rain rang its small bright bells,
And kissed in the back seats of cinemas until
The lights blew up again and made us blink.
Why trouble us? Over the brink
Of a lamplit bridge we have watched together
The river smarting under a lash of many lights,
Felt the pain under our ribs, pain
Making us hold our breath, linked fingers tight,
Shout of the mooned motors, rank smell
Of the river's wounds, while an ocean of footsteps
Dragged about the whorl of our private shell
Whispering the identities, vainly,
The shell murmured our own names only,
Dermot and Grace.

Mile after mile
We fled.
Listen to me now, the quiet man said.

Terse telegram wires urged endlessly
The ying of it, the yang of it,
The death and the erection,
The doomed love of the priestess
Emerging as always from the subsiding wave.

Three times, he said, they had me under the knife,
They said it was gallstone.

Alone.

They have tunnelled the earth and laid us in a tomb.
Aphrodité's lamp is out. Where have we laid
Her clearcut image in this smuttering time?
Grace?

Listen listen listen to me ....

JOHN MONTAGUE (b 1929)

Crossing

Your lithe and golden body
haunts me, as I haunt you:
Corsairs with different freights
who may only cross by chance
    on lucky nights

So our moorings differ.
But scents of your pleasure
still linger disturbingly
around me: fair winds or
    squalls of danger?

There is a way of forgetting you,
but I have forgotten it:
prepared wildly to cut free,
to lurch, like a young man,
    towards ecstasy

Nightly your golden body turns
and turns in my shuddering dream.
Why is my heart never still,
yielding again to the cardinal
    lure of the beautiful?

Age should bring its wisdom
but in your fragrant presence
my truths are one swirling
to a litany – sweet privateer –
    of grateful adulation.

JAMES LIDDY (b 1934)

History

'Tell us, streaming lady,
The cause of your wave travel
Have you left your man
You're certainly in a bad state.'

'I have no husband I have
Not touched a man, Fenian
King of character, I have
The fondness only for your son.'

'To which of my sons, sexual
Blossoming flower, are you giving
Passion – the opportunity
Tell us the whole story, girl.'

'I'll tell you, Finn, it's that
Witty blonde son of yours,
Oisin, with his beautiful
Bright arms that are so long.'

'You're strong for him I see,
Virgin of the unstroked hair,
Why him – there are many
Youths with wealth of skin.'

'The cause is, Fenian father,
I came all that distance
Because his soul's a mansion
His body has a bedroom in

Many a king's chit and courtling
Offered their brownness to get
My love – I never gave my lips
I warmly dreamed of Oisin's.'

Laying my hand on you, Patrick,
It's no shame to a sensual pagan
Every inch of me was panting
For the tresses none had rifled

I clasped her soft sweating hand
Gasped in trembling sweet talk:
'I thank you for saying all that
About me, lovely little lady

You are the nicest girl I've met –
I would prefer to be marched off
By you in chains than by any
Others I've danced with.'

'I have my spell on you, Oisin,
You are a hero and now my husband
Get up on my nag and we'll ride
To the cosmetic suburbs of rejuvenation.'

...

On the horse's back I was put
The untouched feminine in front:
'Let us steal softly out of town,
Oisin, until we reach my place.'

TOGETHERNESS

ANONYMOUS (18th-19th century)

The Coolun *(from the Irish, translated by Douglas Hyde)*

A honey mist on a day of frost, in a dark oak wood,
And love for thee in the heart of me, thou bright white and good,
Thy slender form soft and warm, thy red lips apart,
Thou hast found me, and hast bound me, and put grief in
    my heart.

In fair-green and market, men mark thee, bright, young and
    merry,
Though thou hurt them like foes with the rose of thy blush
    of the berry,
Her cheeks are a poppy, her eye it is Cupid's helper,
But each foolish man dreams that its beams for himself are.

Whoe'er saw the Coolun in a cool dewy meadow
On a morning in summer in sunshine and shadow;
All the young men go wild for her, my childeen, my treasure.
But now let them mope, they've no hope to possess her.

Let us roam, O my darling, afar through the mountains,
Drink milk of the goat, wine and bulcán in fountains,
With music and play every day from my lyre,
And leave to come rest on my breast when you tire.

ANONYMOUS (?18th century)

My Hope, My Love
(from the Irish, translated by Edward Walsh)

My hope, my love, we will go
Into the woods, scattering the dews,
Where we will behold the salmon, and the ousel in its nest,
The deer and the roe-buck calling,
The sweetest bird on the branches warbling,
The cuckoo on the summit of the green hill;
And death shall never approach us
In the bosom of the fragrant wood!

JOHN SWANWICK DRENNAN (1809-1893)

Love

> For love is like a plant that clings
> Most closely unto rugged things,
> And ever clasps with fondest stress
> Deformity and barrenness.

EDWARD DOWDEN (1843-1913)

Turf

> Thank God for simple, honest, close-knit turf,
>> Sound footing for plain feet; nor moss, nor mire;
> No silvery quicksand, no hot sulphurous scurf
>> Flung from a turmoiled fire.
>
> So far your hand has led me: what is worth
>> A question now of all the heavens conceal?
> Here shall we lie, and better love the Earth,
>> And let the planets reel.

FRANCES WYNNE (1866-1893)

Nocturne

> The long day was bright,
> It slowly passed from the purple slopes of the hill;
> And then the night
> Came floating quietly down, and the world grew still.
>
> Now I lie awake,
> The south wind stirs the white curtains to and fro.
> Cries the corncrake
> In fields that stretch by the stream-side, misty and low.
>
> At the meadow's edge
> I know the faint pink clover is heavy with dew.
> Under the hedge
> The speedwell closes its sweet eyes, dreamily blue.

With pursed rosy lips
The baby buds are asleep on the apple tree.
The river slips
Beneath the scarcely swayed willows, on to the sea.

The dark grows, and grows,
But I'm too happy to sleep, and the reason why
No creature knows,
Save certain little brown birds, and my love, and I.

JAMES STEPHENS (?1880-1950)

The Daisies

In the scented bud of the morning – O,
When the windy grass went rippling far,
I saw my dear one walking slow,
In the field where the daisies are.

We did not laugh and we did not speak
As we wandered happily to and fro;
I kissed my dear on either cheek,
In the bud of the morning – O.

A lark sang up from the breezy land,
A lark sang down from the cloud afar,
And she and I went hand in hand
In the field where the daisies are.

AUSTIN CLARKE (1896-1974)

The Straying Student

On a holy day when sails were blowing southward,
A bishop sang the Mass at Inishmore,
Men took one side, their wives were on the other
But I heard the woman coming from the shore:
And wild in despair my parents cried aloud
For they saw the vision draw me to the doorway.

Long had she lived in Rome when Popes were bad,
The wealth of every age she makes her own,
Yet smiled on me in eager admiration,
And for a summer taught me all I know,
Banishing shame with her great laugh that rang
As if a pillar caught it back alone.

I learned the prouder counsel of her throat,
My mind was growing bold as light in Greece;
And when in sleep her stirring limbs were shown,
I blessed the noonday rock that knew no tree:
And for an hour the mountain was her throne,
Although her eyes were bright with mockery.

They say I was sent back from Salamanca
And failed in logic, but I wrote her praise
Nine times upon a college wall in France.
She laid her hand at darkfall on my page
That I might read the heavens in a glance
And I knew every star the Moors had named.

Awake or in my sleep, I have no peace now,
Before the ball is struck, my breath has gone,
And yet I tremble lest she may deceive me
And leave me in this land, where every woman's son
Must carry his own coffin and believe,
In dread, all that the clergy teach the young.

PATRICK KAVANAGH (1904-1967)

Bluebells for Love

There will be bluebells growing under the big trees
And you will be there and I will be there in May;
For some other reason we both will have to delay
The evening in Dunshaughlin – to please
Some imagined relation,
So both of us came to walk through that plantation.

We will be interested in the grass,
In an old bucket-hoop, in the ivy that weaves
Green incongruity among dead leaves,
We will put on surprise at carts that pass –
Only sometimes looking sideways at the bluebells
      in the plantation
And never frighten them with too wild an exclamation.

We will be wise, we will not let them guess
That we are watching them or they will pose
A mere façade like boys
Caught out in virtue's naturalness.
We will not impose on the bluebells in that plantation
Too much of our desire's adulation.

We will have other loves – or so they'll think;
The primroses or the ferns or the briars,
Or even the rusty paling wires,
Or the violets on the sunless sorrel bank.
Only as an aside the bluebells in the plantation
Will mean a thing to our dark contemplation.

We'll know love little by little, glance by glance.
Ah, the clay under these roots is so brown!
We'll steal from Heaven while God is in the town –
I caught an angel smiling in a chance
Look through the tree-trunks of the plantation
As you and I walked slowly to the station.

BRIAN COFFEY (1905-1995)
'The Nicest Phantasies are Shared'

Whence let us go to
what is shared is nicest
and begin

Taking her garments
while she takes his
does not make theirs
a single robe

Their holding hands leaves each
aware of self and other
Their touching skins
breast to mouth mouth to breast
their planting kisses in hair
sunders uniting if he in her
unmatched is by a her in him

And when a pair bereft of day
and movement into night are sunk
how would it suit her her hell him
or suit his will with his hell her

What then is love
for lovers mating
with nought spoiled
though all uprooted
but completing natural skill
forever giving him to her
giving forever her to him
for them joying
in every difference
love decrees.

LOUIS MacNEICE (1907-1963)
Coda

Maybe we knew each other better
When the night was young and unrepeated
And the moon stood still over Jericho.

So much for the past; in the present
There are moments caught between heart-beats
When maybe we know each other better.

But what is that clinking in the darkness?
Maybe we shall know each other better
When the tunnels meet beneath the mountain.

RICHARD MURPHY (b 1927)

Moonshine

To think
I must be alone:
To love
We must be together.

I think I love you
When I'm alone
More than I think of you
When we're together.

I cannot think
Without loving
Or love
Without thinking.

Alone I love
To think of us together
Together I think
I'd love to be alone.

THOMAS KINSELLA (b 1928)

In the Ringwood

As I roved out impatiently
Good Friday with my bride
To drink in the rivered Ringwood
The draughty season's pride
A fell dismay held suddenly
Our feet on the green hillside.

The yellow Spring on Vinegar Hill
The smile of Slaney water,
The wind that swept the Ringwood,
Grew dark with ancient slaughter.
My love cried out and I beheld her
Change to Sorrow's daughter.

'Ravenhair, what rending
Set those red lips a-shriek,
And dealt those locks in black lament
Like blows on your white cheek,
That in your looks outlandishly
Both woe and fury speak?'

As sharp a lance as the fatal heron
There on the sunken tree
Will strike in the stones of the river
Was the gaze she bent on me.
O her robe into her right hand
She gathered grievously.

'Many times the civil lover
Climbed that pleasant place,
Many times despairing
Died in his love's face,
His spittle turned to vinegar,
Blood in his embrace.

'Love that is every miracle
Is torn apart and rent.
The human turns awry
The poles of the firmament.
The fish's bright side is pierced
And good again is spent.

'Though every stem on Vinegar Hill
And stone on the Slaney's bed
And every leaf in the living Ringwood
Builds till it is dead
Yet heart and hand, accomplished,
Destroy until they dread.

'Dread, a grey devourer,
Stalks in the shade of love,
The dark that dogs our feet
Eats what is sickened of.
The End that stalks Beginning
Hurries home its drove.'

I kissed three times her shivering lips.
I drank their naked chill.
I watched the river shining
Where the heron wiped his bill.
I took my love in my icy arms
In the Spring on Ringwood Hill.

JOHN MONTAGUE (b 1929)

That Room

Side by side on the narrow bed
We lay, like chained giants,
Tasting each other's tears, in terror
Of the news which left little to hide
But our two faces that stared
To ritual masks, absurd and flayed.

Rarely in a lifetime comes such news
Shafting knowledge straight to the heart
Making shameless sorrow start –
Not childish tears, querulously vain –
But adult tears that hurt and harm,
Seeping like acid to the bone.

Sound of hooves on the midnight road
Raised a romantic image to mind:
Someone riding late to Marley?
But we must suffer the facts of self;
No one endures a similar fate
And no one will ever know.

What happened in that room
But that when we came to leave
We scrubbed each other's tears
Prepared the usual show. That day
Love's claims made chains of time and place
To bind us together more: equal in adversity.

BRENDAN KENNELLY (b 1936)

We are Living

What is this room
But the moments we have lived in it?
When all due has been paid
To gods of wood and stone
And recognition has been made
Of those who'll breathe here when we are gone
Does it not take its worth from us
Who made it because we were here?

Your words are the only furniture I can remember
Your body the book that told me most.
If this room has a ghost
It will be your laughter in the frank dark
Revealing the world as a room
Loved only for those moments when
We touched the purely human.

I could give water now to thirsty plants,
Dig up the floorboards, the foundation,
Study the worm's confidence,
Challenge his omnipotence
Because my blind eyes have seen through walls
That make safe prisons of the days.

We are living
In ceiling, floor and windows,
We are given to where we have been.
This white door will always open
On what our hands have touched,
Our eyes have seen.

EAVAN BOLAND (b 1944)

Song

Where in blind files
Bats outsleep the frost
Water slips through stones
Too fast, too fast
For ice; afraid he'd slip
By me I asked him first.

Round as a bracelet
Clasping the wet grass,
An adder drowsed by berries
Which change blood to cess;
Dreading delay's venom
I risked the first kiss.

My skirt in my hand,
Lifting the hem high
I forded the river there;
Drops splashed my thigh.
Ahead of me at last
He turned at my cry:

'Look how the water comes
Boldly to my side;
See the waves attempt
What you have never tried.'
He late that night
Followed the leaping tide.

PAUL DURCAN (b 1944)

The Levite and his Concubine at Gibeah

After Paul Durcan left his wife
– Actually she left him but it is more *recherché* to say
That he left her –
Would you believe it but he turned up at our villa
With a woman whom we had never heard of before,
Much less met. To our villa! The Kerrs of Dundalk!
I, Mrs Kerr, with a windowframe around my neck!
You will not believe it but he actually asked me
To put him up for the night – and his friend –
A slip of a thing, half his age.
I said that I would but in separate bedrooms.
This is a family home – I had to remind him.
I resented having to remind him.

The pair of them proceeded to squat in silence
In the living room for what was left of the evening,
So that I could not even switch on the television.
As a consequence I missed *Twin Peaks*.
What got up my nose
Was that she sat on the step of the fireplace
On a cushion from our sofa thrown down by him
With her hands joined around his knees:
Himself sitting in my husband's armchair
As if he owned it – without so much as a 'May I?'

She was got up in a loudspoken yellow dress
And those precious little hands of hers around his knees
As if his knees were pillows;
Her face a teatowel of holy innocence
As if margarine would not melt in her tonsils.
I would go so far as to say that it was indelicate –
The way she had her hands joined around his knees.

As soon as I began to yawn, he began to speak:
Holding forth until three o'clock in the a.m.
On what he called his 'Theory of Peripeteia' –
A dog's dinner of gibberish about the philosophical significance
Of 'not caring being the secret to transforming misfortune'.
Finally I stood up and declared 'Peripeteia, Goodnight'.
I installed the pair of them in separate bedrooms.
I left my own bedroom door open.

I fell asleep about five.
When I knocked him up for breakfast
She answered the door. I was that indignant
That when they came down for breakfast
I gave them porridge – like it or lump it.
I did not utter one word to them
Until they had finished.
Then I took him aside and I let him have it:
Now listen to me Paul Durcan:
You may be a poet and a Levite
But you will not take advantage of me,
Get yourself and your – your – your concubine
Out of my Dundalk villa.
How dare a woman wear a loudspoken yellow dress –
When you set foot in Gibeah next time
Do not ever Durcan my doorstep again.

Know what his response was? To ask me
If he might borrow my Shell Guide and my donkey?
To be rid of him I gave in – more fool I.
He shimmied out the door singing to himself:
'We borrowed the loan of Kerr's big ass
To go to Dundalk with butter ...'

Know what he did then? He went down to that old peasant
In the lane at the end of the avenue – Kavanagh –
Who goes about the town always with his socks down
Because he used play football for Mucker-Rotterdam:
Kavanagh with that – that ridiculous –
That – that vulgar –
That – that gross

Brass knocker on his front door.

JOAN McBREEN (b 1945)

This Moon, These Stars

Something is changing.
There is a September stillness in the garden.

We have woken in this bed for years.
You have followed me into my poems,
my dreams, my past, to places I scarcely
know of myself.
I called one evening
from our back doorstep. 'Look,' I said,
'look at this moon.' We stood there
in silence, not touching, not knowing
what to say.

We have been together many days, many nights.
These stars have come out
over us again and again.

Here is the life we are living,
not on a windswept beach, not in vast
city streets, not in a strange country
but here, where we have chosen to be.

I look at myself in the glass, at the woman
I am.

I think of our days, our years running on
into each other.

What will we say,
what will we know.

Separate, together,
will we find the right way, the dream
neither of us can explain.

I pull the living room curtains together.
The garden is around us,
still above us are the stars,
light and indestructible.

THEO DORGAN (b 1953)

All Souls' Eve

Deirid lucht léinn gur chloíte an galar an grá ...
Nuair a théas sé fá'n chroí cha scaoiltear as é go brách.

Once a year in a troubled sleep
That room stands drenched in light
Where I sit and watch us both asleep
In a cold sweat of fright.

A high room where the boards creak
The skylight faced with frost
Our bodies interlaced in sleep
And the world long lost.
Beside the bed my blue jeans
Lie crumpled in your dress
Dawn light coming in as we
Unconsciously caress.

The germ of death is in that dream
There in our mingled breath
There in our silence and our speech
– as when you moan *not yet*.
We lie in the breath of lovers lost
To the world since time began
Their souls the patterns in the frost
As you turn beneath my hand.

Once a year in a troubled sleep
I watch until we wake
... this is a vigil that I keep
And never must forsake
Until slow bells break
From a world long lost
Sleep-drugged lovers
To a city gripped in frost.

There is no time and all time
As we surface to a kiss
What we were before we died
A game compared to this.

No world and a whole world
In an innocent caress
Never again the same world
We leave when we undress.

The learned men say that love
Is a killing disease.
When it goes to the heart
It will never come out again.

MARY O'MALLEY (b 1954)

Aftermath
For Mike

Last night I looked at you,
A stark man in this grey country
Of short days and long nightfalls.
I watched and marvelled
That you should still be here,
For I had not seen you much
In the storms of these past years.

Time and God and bureaucrats
Have pared us both down
To some of our essentials,
With deft little secateurs
Or blunt edgeless implements,
Such as are sought in murder hunts.

Each inflicted its own pain
As it peeled back, gouged
Or merely hacked away
To reach and reveal a deeper layer,
Here a terra cotta shard
Of smashed solicitude,
There a flint of fear,

Perhaps even a purple thread,
Last remnant of some glorious bolt
Of desire. Such delvings and exhumations
Seldom yield the unbroken,
Though sometimes beautiful tokens
Are taken out of their darkness
To be exposed to the light in museums.

They have left me with furrows
And ridges that no coyness
Can rechristen laughter lines.
Yet you are still here;
And I watching
Wondered if I would ever know
This defined and distant man
That I have lived beside
As I knew the boy
The instant the air shifted between us,
Moments after we met.

ANDREW ELLIOTT (date unknown)

Eavesdropping

With my eyes closed I am listening
To her breathing after she has gone to sleep
It is like slipping a piece of tissue paper
Between her head and the pillow –
Into that middle distance
Where her thoughts ripple and settle
And leave an imprint of the day.
If she opens one eye it is to say
'Can't you ever leave me alone?'

FRUSTRATION
&
JEALOUSY

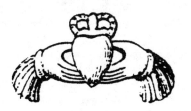

ANONYMOUS (9th-10th century)

A Love-Song *(from the Irish, translated by Brendan Kennelly)*

> Such a heart!
> Should he leave, how I'd miss him.
> Jewel, acorn, youth.
> Kiss him!

ANONYMOUS (15th-16th century)

The Kiss *(from the Irish, translated by the Earl of Longford)*

> Oh, keep your kisses, young provoking girl!
>   I find no taste in any maiden's kiss.
> Although your teeth be whiter than the pearl,
>   I will not drink at fountains such as this.
>
> I know a man whose wife did kiss my mouth
>   With kiss more honeyed than the honeycomb.
> And never another's kiss can slake my drought
>   After that kiss, till judgment hour shall come.
>
> Till I do gaze on her for whom I long,
>   If ever God afford such grace to men,
> I would not love a woman old or young,
>   Till she do kiss me as she kissed me then.

ANONYMOUS (?16th century)

Love is a Mortal Disease
(from the Irish, translated by Eleanor Hull)

> My grief and my pain! a mortal disease is love,
> Woe, woe unto him who must prove it a month or even a day,
> It hath broken my heart, and my bosom is burdened with sighs,
> From dreaming of her gentle sleep hath forsaken mine eyes.

I met with the fairy host at the liss beside Ballyfinnane;
I asked them had they a herb for the curing of love's
    cruel pain.
They answered me softly and mildly, with many a pitying tone,
'When this torment comes into the heart it never goes
    out again.'

It seems to me long till the tide washes up on the strand;
It seems to me long till the night shall fade into day;
It seems to me long till the cocks crow on every hand;
And rather than the world were I close beside my love.

Do not marry the grey old man, but marry the young
    man, dear;
Marry the lad who loves you, my grief, though he live
    not out the year;
Youthful you are, and kind, but your mind is not yet come
    to sense,
And if you live longer, the lads will be following you.

My woe and my plight! where tonight is the snowdrift
    and frost?
Or even I and my love together breasting the waves of the sea;
Without bark, without boat, without any vessel with me,
But I to be swimming, and my arm to be circling her waist!

ANONYMOUS (17th century)

Hate Goes Just as Far as Love
(from the Irish, translated by Brendan Kennelly)

    Woman full of hate for me
        Do you not recall the night
    When we together, side by side,
            Knew love's delight?

    If you remembered woman, how,
        While the sun lost its heat,
    You and I grew hot –
            But why repeat?

Do you recall my lips on yours,
       Soft words you said,
And how you laid your curving arm
       Under my head?

Or do you remember, O sweet shape,
       How you whispered passionately
That God Almighty had never made
       A man like me?

I gave all my heart to you,
       Gave all, yet could not give enough;
Now, I've your hate. O skin like flowers,
       This hate goes just as far as love.

If a man believes he loves a woman
       And that she loves him too,
Let him know one thing for certain –
       It is not true.

ANONYMOUS (17th-19th century)

The Poor Girl's Meditation

(from the Irish, translated by Padraic Colum)

I am sitting here,
Since the moon rose in the night;
Kindling a fire,
And striving to keep it alight:
The folk of the house are lying
In slumber deep;
The cocks will be crowing soon:
The whole of the land is asleep.

May I never leave this world
Until my ill-luck is gone;
Till I have cows and sheep,
And the lad that I love for my own:
I would not think it long,
The night I would lie at his breast,
And the daughters of spite, after that,
Might say the thing they liked best.

Love covers up hate,
If a girl have beauty at all:
On a bed that was narrow and high,
A three-month I lie by the wall:
When I bethought on the lad
That I left on the brow of the hill,
I wept from dark until dark
And my cheeks have the tear-tracks still.

And, O, young lad that I love,
I am no mark for your scorn:
All you can say of me
Is undowered I was born:
And if I've no fortune in hand,
Nor cattle nor sheep of my own,
This I can say, O lad,
I am fitted to lie my lone!

ESTHER JOHNSON ['STELLA'] (1681-1728)

On Jealousy

O shield me from his rage, celestial powers!
This tyrant that embitters all my hours.
Ah, Love! you've poorly played the hero's part,
You conquered, but you can't defend my heart.
When first I bent beneath your gentle reign,
I thought this monster banished from your train:
But you would raise him to support your throne,
And now he claims your empire as his own;
Or tell me, tyrants, have you both agreed
That where one reigns, the other shall succeed?

ANONYMOUS (18th-19th century)

The Red Man's Wife (*from the Irish, translated by Douglas Hyde*)

'Tis what they say,
Thy little heel fits in a shoe.
'Tis what they say,
Thy little mouth kisses well, too.
'Tis what they say,
Thousand loves that you leave me to rue;
That the tailor went the way
That the wife of the Red man knew.

Nine months did I spend
In a prison penned tightly and bound;
Bolts on my smalls
And a thousand locks frowning around;
But o'er the tide
I would leap with the leap of a swan,
Could I once set my side
By the bride of the Red-haired man.

I thought, O my life,
That one house between us, love, would be;
And I thought I should find
You once coaxing my child on your knee;
But now the curse of the High One,
On him let it be,
And on all of the band of the liars
Who put silence between you and me.

There grows a tree in the garden
With blossoms that tremble and shake,
I lay my hands on its bark
And I feel that my heart must break.
On one wish alone
My soul through the long months ran,
One little kiss
From the wife of the Red-haired man.

But the day of doom shall come,
And hills and harbours be rent;
A mist shall fall on the sun
From the dark clouds heavily sent;
The sea shall be dry,
And earth under mourning and ban;
Then loud shall he cry
For the wife of the Red-haired man.

BRIAN MERRIMAN (?1749-1805)

Against Clerical Celibacy *from* Cúirt an Mhean Oíche
(from the Irish, translated by Arland Ussher)

We know it is true there are few but hate
The lonely life and the celibate state;
Is it fair to condemn them to mope and moan,
Is it fair to force them to lie alone,
To bereave of issue a sturdy band
The fruit of whose loins might free the land?
Though some of them ever were grim and gruff,
Intractable, sullen and stern and tough,
Crabbed and cross, unkind and cold,
Surly and wont to scowl and scold,
Many are made of warmer clay,
Affectionate, ardent, kind and gay;
It's often a women got land or wealth,
Store or stock from a priest by stealth,
Many's the case I call to mind
Of clergymen who were slyly kind,
I could show you women who were their flames
And their children reared beneath false names;
And often I must lament in vain
How they waste their strength on the old and the plain.
It's often I've asked and sought in vain
What is the use of the rule insane
That marriage has closed to the clerical clan
In the church of our fathers since first it began.
It's a melancholy sight to a needy maid
Their comely faces and forms displayed,

Their hips and thighs so broad and round,
Their buttocks and breasts that in flesh abound,
Their lustrous looks and their lusty limbs,
Their fair, fresh features, their smooth, soft skins,
Their strength and stature, their force and fire,
Their craving curbed and uncooled desire.
They eat and drink of the fat of the land,
They've wealth and comfort at their command,
They sleep on beds of the softest down,
They've ease and leisure their lot to crown.
They commence in manhood's prime and flood
And well we know that they're flesh and blood!
If I thought that sexless saints they were
Or holy angels, I would not care,
But they're lusty lads with a crave unsated
In slothful sleep, and the maids unmated
While marriageable maids their plight deplore
Waiting unwooed through this senseless law;
'Tis a baleful ban to an hapless race
And beneath its sway we decay apace.

GEORGE DARLEY (1795-1846)

Last Night

I sat with one I love last night,
She sang to me an olden strain;
In former times it woke delight.
Last night – but pain.
Last night we saw the stars rise,
But clouds soon dimmed the ether blue:
And when we sought each other's eyes
Tears dimmed them too!

We paced alone our favourite walk
But paced in silence broken-hearted:
Of old we used to smile and talk.
Last night – we parted.

GEORGE DARLEY

Siren Chorus

Troop home to silent grots and caves,
      Troop home! and mimic as you go
The mournful winding of the waves
      Which to their dark abysses flow.

At this sweet hour all things beside
      In amorous pairs to covert creep,
The swans that brush the evening tide
      Homeward in snowy couples keep.

In his green den the murmuring seal
      Close by his sleek companion lies,
While singly we to bedward steal,
      And close in fruitless sleep our eyes.

In bowers of love men take their rest,
      In loveless bowers we sigh alone,
With bosom-friends are others blest,
      But we have none, but we have none!

ARTHUR O'SHAUGHNESSY (1844-1881)

Song

I made another garden, yea,
      For my new love;
I left the dead rose where it lay,
      And set the new above.
Why did the summer not begin?
      Why did my heart not haste?
My old love came and walked therein,
      And laid the garden waste.

She entered with her weary smile,
      Just as of old;
She looked around a little while,
      And shivered at the cold.

Her passing touch was death to all,
  Her passing look a blight:
She made the white rose-petals fall,
  And turned the red rose white.

Her pale robe, clinging to the grass,
  Seemed like a snake
That bit the grass and ground, alas!
  And a sad trail did make.
She went slowly up to the gate;
  And there, just as of yore,
She turned back at the last to wait,
  And say farewell once more.

ANONYMOUS (?18th century)

What is Love? *(from the Irish, translated by Alfred Perceval Graves)*

A love all-commanding, all-withstanding
Through a year is my love;
A grief darkly hiding, starkly biding
Without let or remove;
Of strength a sharp sharing, past sustaining
Wheresoever I rove,
A force still extending without ending
Before and around and above.

Of Heaven 'tis the brightest amazement,
The blackest abasement of Hell,
A struggle for breath with a spectre,
In nectar a choking to death;
'Tis a race with Heaven's lightning and thunder,
Then champion feats under Moyle's water:
'Tis pursuing the cuckoo, the wooing
Of echo, the Rock's airy daughter.

Till my red lips turn ashen,
My light limbs grow leaden,
My heart loses motion,
In Death my eyes deaden,

So is my love and my passion,
So is my ceaseless devotion
To her to whom I gave them
To her who will not have them.

OSCAR WILDE (1854-1900)

Remorse
(A Study in Saffron)

I love your topaz-coloured eyes
    That light with blame these midnight streets,
I love your body when it lies
    Like amber on the silken sheets.

I love the honey-coloured hair
    That ripples to your ivory hips;
I love the languid listless air
    With which you kiss my boyish lips.

I love the brows that bend above
    Those eyelids of chalcedony:
But most of all, my love! I love
    Your beautiful fierce chastity!

WILLIAM BUTLER YEATS (1865-1939)

No Second Troy

Why should I blame her that she filled my days
With misery, or that she would of late
Have taught to ignorant men most violent ways,
Or hurled the little streets upon the great,
Had they but courage equal to desire?
What could have made her peaceful with a mind
That nobleness made simple as a fire,
With beauty like a tightened bow, a kind
That is not natural in an age like this,
Being high and solitary and most stern?
Why, what could she have done, being what she is?
Was there another Troy for her to burn?

DORA SIGERSON SHORTER (1866-1918)
The Lone of Soul

The world has many lovers, but the one
She loves the best is he within whose heart
She but half-reigning queen and mistress is;
Whose lonely soul for ever stands apart.

Who from her face will ever turn away,
Who but half-hearing listens to her voice,
Whose heart beats to her passion, but whose soul
Within her presence never will rejoice.

What land has let the dreamer from its gates.
What face beloved hides from him away?
A dreamer outcast from some world of dreams.
He goes for ever lonely on his way

The wedded body and the single soul,
Beside his mate he shall most mateless stand.
For ever to dream of that unseen face
For ever to sigh for that enchanted land.

Like a great pine upon some Alpine height
Torn by the winds and bent beneath the snow,
Half overthrown by icy avalanche.
The lone of soul throughout the world must go.

Alone among his kind he stands alone,
Torn by the passions of his own strange heart,
Stoned by continual wreckage of his dreams,
He in the crowd for ever is apart.

Like the great pine that, rocking no sweet nest,
Swings no young birds to sleep upon the bough,
But where the raven only comes to croak,
'There lives no man more desolate than thou!'
So goes the lone of soul amid the world,
No love upon his breast, with singing, cheers.
But Sorrow builds her home within his heart,
And, nesting there, will rear her brood of tears.

PATRICK PEARSE (1897-1916)

Ideal *(from the Irish, translated by Thomas MacDonagh)*

Naked I saw thee,
O beauty of beauty!
And I blinded my eyes
For fear I should flinch.

I heard thy music,
O sweetness of sweetness!
And I shut my ears
For fear I should fail.

I kissed thy lips
O sweetness of sweetness!
And I hardened my heart
For fear of my ruin.

I blinded my eyes
And my ears I shut,
I hardened my heart
And my love I quenched.

I turned my back
On the dream I had shaped,
And to this road before me
My face I turned.

I set my face
To the road here before me,
To the work that I see,
To the death that I shall meet.

SIDNEY ROYSE LYSAGHT (?-1941)
The Penalty of Love

If love should count you worthy, and should deign
One day to seek your door and be your guest,
Pause! 'ere you draw the bolt and bid him rest,
If in your old content you would remain.
For not alone he enters: in his train
Are angels of the mists, the lovely guest,
Dreams of the unfulfilled and unpossessed
And sorrow, and life's immemorial pain
He wakes desires you never may forget,
He shows you stars you never saw before,
He makes you share with him for evermore
The burden of the world's divine regret.
How wise you were to open not! – and yet,
How poor if you should turn him from the door.

BLANAID SALKELD (1880-1959)
Terenure

I laughed at the lovers I passed
Two and two in the shadows –
I, solitary as one old horse I saw
Alone in the meadows.
The lovers so many I passed,
In mute embraces;
A roadside flower, joy,
In the hid places.
I wondered, sure, to notice joy
As common as a weed –
Out of my loneliness wondering,
Laughing, indeed.
I loved all the lovers I passed
Two and two, in the shadows:
I, solitary as one old horse, was standing
Alone in the meadows.

AUSTIN CLARKE (1896-1974)

Celibacy

On a brown isle of Lough Corrib,
When clouds were bare as branch
And water had been thorned
By colder days, I sank
In torment of her side;
But still that woman stayed,
For eye obeys the mind.

Bedraggled in the briar
And grey fire of the nettle,
Three nights, I fell, I groaned
On the flagstone of help
To pluck her from my body;
For servant ribbed with hunger
May climb his rungs to God.

Eyelid stood back in sleep,
I saw what seemed an Angel:
Dews dripped from those bright feet.
But, O, I knew the stranger
By her deceit and, tired
All night by tempting flesh,
I wrestled her in hair-shirt.

On pale knees in the dawn,
Parting the straw that wrapped me,
She sank until I saw
The bright roots of her scalp.
She pulled me down to sleep,
But I fled as the Baptist
To thistle and to reed.

The dragons of the Gospel
Are cast by bell and crook;
But fiery as the frost
Or bladed light, she drew
The reeds back, when I fought
The arrow-headed airs
That darken on the water.

SEAMUS HEANEY (b 1939)

A Dream of Jealousy

Walking with you and another lady
In wooded parkland, the whispering grass
Ran its fingers through our guessing silence
And the trees opened into a shady
Unexpected clearing where we sat down.
I think the candour of the light dismayed us.
We talked about desire and being jealous,
Our conversation a loose single gown
Or a white picnic tablecloth spread out
Like a book of manners in the wilderness.
'Show me,' I said to our companion, 'what
I have much coveted, your breast's mauve star.'
And she consented. O neither these verses
Nor my prudence, love, can heal your wounded stare.

ROSITA BOLAND (b 1965)

Fireworks

We sat with our arms held tight
Around each other
While we watched the fireworks blow open
In huge, coloured dandelion puffs
That burst and fell like melting tinsel
Against the backdrop of an August night.

I knew that those nights
Were climbing into bed beside us,
Staining the sheets with their dark colours
I kept reaching out for you,
But my arms were burning only in a night
That gathered me into an empty embrace
Until sliding quietly away into dawn,
Leaving its indigo shadows smeared
Beneath the ashy embers of my eyes.

That same year,
You tossed me away with the casual, easy grace
That came so fluidly to your deft hands
And sent me spinning through the Autumn
Exploding in savage reds and orange
That came too late to scald you.

WOMEN

ANONYMOUS (13th-17th century)

My Love, Oh, She is My Love

(from the Irish, translated by Douglas Hyde)

My love, oh, she is my love,
   The woman who is most for destroying me;
   Dearer is she from making me ill
   Than the woman who would be for making me well.

She is my treasure, oh, she is my treasure,
   The woman of the grey eye, she like the rose,
   A woman who would not place a hand beneath my head,
   A woman who would not be with me for gold.

She is my affection, oh, she is my affection,
   The woman who left no strength in me;
   A woman who would not breathe a sigh after me,
   A woman who would not raise a stone at my tomb.

She is my secret love, oh, she is my secret love,
   A woman who tells me nothing;
   A woman who would not breathe a sigh after me,
   A woman who would not shed tears.

It is she ruined my heart,
   And left a sigh for ever in me.
   Unless this evil be raised off my heart,
   I shall not be well for ever.

GERALD FITZGERALD, 4TH EARL OF DESMOND (d 1398

Against Blame of Woman

(from the Irish, translated by the Earl of Longford)

Speak not ill of womankind.
'Tis no wisdom if you do.
You that fault in women find,
I would not be praised of you.

Sweetly speaking, witty, clear,
Tribe most lovely to my mind,
Blame of such I hate to hear.
Speak not ill of womankind.

Bloody treason, murderous act,
Not by women were designed,
Bells o'erthrown nor churches sacked.
Speak not ill of womankind.

Bishop, King upon his throne,
Primate skilled to loose and bind,
Sprung of women every one!
Speak not ill of womankind.

For a brave young fellow long
Hearts of women oft have pined.
Who would dare their love to wrong
Speak not ill of womankind.

Paunchy greybeards never more
Hope to please a woman's mind
Poor young chieftains they adore!"
Speak not ill of womankind.

JOHN KELLY (1680-1751)

On Beauty

Beauty gilds the blushing morn,
Hangs the dew-drop on the thorn,
Paints the rose in richest bloom,
Fills the air with sweet perfume:
    But sweet perfume,
    Nor rose in bloom,
    Nor dew-drop bright,
    Nor morning light,
    In charms can vie
    With woman's eye.
In woman's eye we raptured view
Beauty at once, and pleasure too.

OLIVER GOLDSMITH (1728-1774)

Stanzas on Woman

When lovely Woman stoops to folly,
   And finds too late that men betray,
What charm can soothe her melancholy,
   What art can wash her guilt away?

The only art her guilt to cover,
   To hide her shame from every eye,
To give repentance to her lover,
   And wring his bosom – is, to die.

PADRAIC FALLON (1905-1975)

Women

The pity of it. Not to love
All the love we lean upon;
Always to be at some remove,
Always to be drawn
Towards the overwhelming one
We must need alone.

O loneliness – We are born to them:
As mothers they mother us;
We break the navel cord like a limb
That as lovers they may love us:
But recover us
And leave them for our loveliness.

Rest, says the earth. And a woman delicately
says 'It is here, it is in my arms somewhere'
But a woman is a lie
And I have a tower to climb, the tower of me,
And a quarrel to settle with the sky
But 'rest' says the woman. 'O lean back more
I am a wife and a mother's knee,
I am the end of every tower.'

MARRIAGE

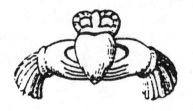

ANONYMOUS (?16th century)

Woman Don't Be Troublesome
(from the Irish, translated by Augustus Young)

Woman, don't be troublesome,
though your husband I may be;
our two minds were once at one,
why withdraw your hand from me.

Put your mouth of strawberry
on my mouth, cream is your cheek;
wind round white arms about me,
and do not go back to sleep.

Stay with me my flighty maid,
and be done with betrayal;
tonight this bed is wellmade,
let us toss it without fail.

Shut your eyes to other men,
no more women will I see:
the milkwhite tooth of passion
is between us – or should be.

MARY BARBER (1690-1757)

Advice to Her Son on Marriage
from The Conclusion of a Letter to the Rev. Mr C–

When you gain her affection, take care to preserve it;
Lest others persuade her, you do not deserve it.
Still study to heighten the joys of her life;
Not treat her the worse, for her being your wife.
If in judgment she errs, set her right, without pride:
'Tis the province of insolent fools, to deride.
A husband's first praise is a Friend and Protector:

Then change not these titles, for Tyrant and Hector.
Let your person be neat, unaffectedly clean,
Though alone with your wife the whole day you remain.
Choose books, for her study, to fashion her mind,
To emulate those who excelled of her kind.
Be religion the principal care of your life,
As you hope to be blest in your children and wife:
So you, in your marriage, shall gain its true end;
And find, in your wife, a Companion and Friend.

ANONYMOUS (c 1785)

The Palatine's Daughter (from the Irish,
translated by Donal O'Sullivan)

As I roved out one evening through
    The groves of Ballyseedy,
Whom should I meet on a cool retreat
    But an Irish Palatine's daughter?
She asked my name and station O!
    Or where was my dwelling arbour?
Or would I come along with her
    To see her own dear father?
I said I was a rakish lad,
    In Currans I was in sarvice.

'If you forsake the Mass and sacraments
    You'll get me and my portion,
As I have done in person and
    My forefathers before me.
You'll get gold and silver O!
    And land without tax or charges,
And a letter from Mister Oliver
    My father's unfit for sarvice,
And a pretty lass to wed with you,
    If you choose a Palatine's daughter.'

I courteously saluted her
       And twice I kissed my darling:
'And if I go home along with you
       Shall I get you as my partner?'
She said, 'A thousand welcomes O!
       And be not the least alarmed,
You'll have my mother's blessing and
       Best wishes of my father,
You'll get stock and property,
       And we'll be happy ever after.'

And now my song is ended and
       My pen is out of order,
She brought this handsome young man
       In presence of her father.
They agreed and soon get married O!
       And then he became master,
He got his landed property,
       His haggard and his barn,
And then he made a Catholic
       Of the Irish Palatine's daughter.

OSCAR WILDE (1854-1900)

To My Wife

With a copy of my poems

I can write no stately poem
       As a prelude to my lay;
From a poet to a poem
       I would dare to say;

For if of these fallen petals
       One to you seem fair,
Love will waft it till it settles
       On your hair.

And when wind and winter harden
       All the loveless land,
It will whisper of the garden,
       You will understand.

KATHARINE TYNAN (1861-1931)

Any Wife

Nobody knows but you and I, my dear,
And the stars, the spies of God, that lean and peer,
Those nights when you and I in a narrow strait
Were under the ships of God and desolate.
In extreme pain, in uttermost agony,
We bore the cross for each other, you and I,
When, through the darkest hour, the night of dread,
I suffered and you supported my head.

Ties that bind us together for life and death,
O hard-set fight in the darkness, shuddering breath,
Because a man can only bear as he may,
And find no tears for easing, the woman's way,
Anguish of pity, sharp in the heart like a sword;
Dost Thou not know, O Lord? Thou knowest, Lord,
What we endured for each other: our wounds were red
When he suffered and I supported his head.

Grief that binds us closer than smile or kiss,
Into the pang God slips the exquisite bliss.
You were my angel and I your angel, as he,
The angel, comforted Christ in His agony,
Lifting Him up from the earth that His blood made wet,
Pillowing the Holy Head, dabbled in sweat,
Thou who wert under the scourges knowest to prove
Love by its pangs, love that endures for love.

WILLIAM BUTLER YEATS (1865-1939)

from **The Gift of Harun Al-Rashid**

> Upon a moonless night
> I sat where I could watch her sleeping form,
> And wrote by candle-light; but her form moved,
> And fearing that my light disturbed her sleep
> I rose that I might screen it with a cloth.
> I heard her voice, 'Turn that I may expound
> What's bowed your shoulder and made pale your cheek';
> And saw her sitting upright on the bed;
> Or was it she that spoke or some great Djinn?
> I say that a Djinn spoke. A livelong hour
> She seemed the learned man and I the child;
> Truths without father came, truths that no book
> Of all the uncounted books that I have read,
> Nor thought out of her mind or mine begot,
> Self-born, high-born, and solitary truths,
> Those terrible implacable straight lines
> Drawn through the wandering vegetative dream,
> Even those truths that when my bones are dust
> Must drive the Arabian host.

> The voice grew still,
> And she lay down upon her bed and slept,
> But woke at the first gleam of day, rose up
> And swept the house and sang about her work
> In childish ignorance of all that passed.
> A dozen nights of natural sleep, and then
> When the full moon swam to its greatest height
> She rose, and with her eyes shut fast in sleep
> Walked through the house. Unnoticed and unfelt
> I wrapped her in a hooded cloak, and she,
> Half running, dropped at the first ridge of the desert
> And there marked out those emblems on the sand
> That day by day I study and marvel at,

With her white finger. I led her home asleep
And once again she rose and swept the house
In childish ignorance of all that passed.
Even to-day, after some seven years
When maybe thrice in every moon her mouth
Murmured the wisdom of the desert Djinns,
She keeps that ignorance, nor has she now
That first unnatural interest in my books.
It seems enough that I am there; and yet,
Old fellow-student, whose most patient ear
Heard all the anxiety of my passionate youth,
It seems I must buy knowledge with my peace.
What if she lose her ignorance and so
Dream that I love her only for the voice,
That every gift and every word of praise
Is but a payment for that midnight voice
That is to age what milk is to a child?
Were she to lose her love, because she had lost
Her confidence in mine, or even lose
Its first simplicity, love, voice and all,
All my fine feathers would be plucked away
And I left shivering. The voice has drawn
A quality of wisdom from her love's
Particular quality. The signs and shapes;
All those abstractions that you fancied were
From the great Treatise of Parmenides;
All, all those gyres and cubes and midnight things
Are but a new expression of her body
Drunk with the bitter sweetness of her youth.
And now my utmost mystery is out.
A woman's beauty is a storm-tossed banner;
Under it wisdom stands, and I alone –
Of all Arabia's lovers I alone –
Nor dazzled by the embroidery, nor lost
In the confusion of its night-dark folds,
Can hear the armed man speak.

LYNN DOYLE (1873-1961)

A Widower

Get me a sup of port in a clean glass,
An' a half-one of malt – the fifteen year.
I'm going out now to fetch a pretty lass,
An' we'll drink each other's health in here.

She's marryin' my son, the eldest chap,
So say nothing, an' let nobody see;
For cash an' land are tumbling in his lap
An' I brought him into the world; but she'd rather have me.

Him an' his cigarettes, an' his malted milk!
An' his sports coat, an' his trousers with a crease
He'll doll her up with a fur, an' stockings of silk,
An' do as he's told; but a girl doesn't marry for peace.

A woman likes a man that can act the man,
That'll drive labour, an' put away, an' spend,
An' fight for her brats; an' goes on the ran-dan,
But comes back to her in the end.

I've sized this lassie up an' that's her sort;
She's full of blood an' fun, an' as true as steel;
When I looked her first in the eye she looked back sport,
When the horse ran away she never let one squeal.

Old an' all as I am I could gunk him yet,
An' raise a son that I'll swear would bring me pride;
But one day she'd know affronted love, an' would regret,
An' I'd be girnin' hate by the fireside.

So we'll drink together, her an' me, an' say good-bye;
I'll give her a hug an' a kiss an' go my way;
For young notions sort badly with sixty-five,
An' I know my place an' have had my day.

JAMES STEPHENS (c 1880-1950)
Nóra Críona

I have looked him round and looked him through,
Know everything that he would do
In such a case, in such a case,
And when a frown comes on his face
I dream of it, and when a smile
I trace its sources in a while.
He cannot do a thing but I
Peep to find the reason why,
For I love him, and I seek,
Every evening in the week,
To peep behind his frowning eye
With little query, little pry,
And make him if a woman can
Happier than any man.
Yesterday he gripped her tight
And cut her throat – and serve her right!

L. A. G. STRONG (1896-1958)
The Brewer's Man

Have I a wife? Bedam I have!
But we was badly mated.
I hit her a great clout one night
And now we're separated.

And mornin's going to me work
I meets her on the quay:
'Good mornin' to you, ma'am!' says I,
'To hell with ye!' says she.

GEORGE BUCHANAN (1904-1989)

Song for Straphangers

I bought a red-brick villa
and dug the garden round
because a young girl smiled in June:
in August we were bound
by a marriage vow
and then till now
I count up every pound.

I count up every penny,
I work and never cease,
because a young girl smiled in June
and there is no release.
Sometimes I swear
it's most unfair.
Sometimes I feel at peace ...

FERGUS ALLEN (b 1921)

The Fall

The Garden of Eden (described in the Bible)
Was Guinness's Brewery (mentioned by Joyce),
Where innocent Adam and Eve were created
And dwelt from necessity rather than choice;

For nothing existed but Guinness's Brewery,
Guinness's Brewery occupied all,
Guinness's Brewery everywhere, anywhere
Woe that expulsion succeeded the Fall!

The ignorant pair were encouraged in drinking
Whatever they fancied whenever they could,
Except for the porter or stout which embodied
Delectable knowledge of Evil and Good.

In Guinness's Brewery, innocent, happy,
They tended the silos and coppers and vats,
They polished the engines and coopered the barrels
And even made pets of the Brewery rats.

One morning while Adam was brooding and brewing
It happened that Eve had gone off on her own,
When a serpent like ivy slid up to her softly
And murmured seductively, Are we alone?

O Eve, said the serpent, I beg you to sample
A bottle of Guinness's excellent stout,
Whose nutritive qualities no one can question
And stimulant properties no one can doubt;

It's tonic, enlivening, strengthening, heartening,
Loaded with vitamins, straight from the wood,
And further enriched with the not undesirable
Lucrative knowledge of Evil and Good.

So Eve was persuaded and Adam was tempted,
They fell and they drank and continued to drink
(Their singing and dancing and shouting and prancing
Prevented the serpent from sleeping a wink).

Alas, when the couple had finished a barrel
And swallowed the final informative drops,
They looked at each other and knew they were naked
And covered their intimate bodies with hops.

The anger and rage of the Lord were appalling,
He wrathfully cursed them for taking to drink
And hounded them out of the Brewery, followed
By beetles (magenta) and elephants (pink).

The crapulous couple emerged to discover
A universe full of diseases and crimes,
Where porter could only be purchased for money
In specified places at specified times.

And now in this world of confusion and error
Our only salvation and hope is to try
To threaten and bargain our way into Heaven
By drinking the heavenly Brewery dry.

LELAND BARDWELL (b 1928)
Lullaby

Lullaby sing lullaby
To my sweet baby in his cradle
Your daddy's gone but what is worse
I wish that I had left him first
Oh lullaby, sing lullaby

EVANGELINE PATERSON (b 1928)
Wife to Husband

you are a person
like a tree
standing like rock
moving like water

you show me how
to hold like a root
and how to dance
in a changing rhythm

you hold me close
in a singing stillness
you rock me slow
in a crazy wind

you show me a height
that I may grow to
you cover the sky
with stars and branches

you lose your leaves
without complaining
you know there will be
another spring

you stand like rock
you move like water
you are a person
like a tree

JAMES SIMMONS (b 1933)

A Song

With your clothes on the chair
and one white sheet above you
I have no need of words
to explain why I love you.
Every touch of delight
through the long wedding night
Is defining our love.
With this kiss I thee wed.

If our luck should run out
and love withers and dies, love,
don't try out of kindness
to save me with this love
You won't need to explain
that I'm single again
and the marriage is done
when your kiss says goodbye.

SEAMUS HEANEY (b 1939)

Poem for Marie

Love, I shall perfect for you the child
Who diligently potters in my brain
Digging with heavy spade till sods were piled
Or puddling through muck in a deep drain.

Yearly I would sow my yard-long garden.
I'd strip a layer of sods to build the wall
That was to exclude sow and picking hen.
Yearly, admitting these the sods would fall,

Or in the sucking clabber I would splash
Delightedly and dam the flowing drain
But always my bastions of clay and muck
Would burst before the rising autumn rain.

Love, you shall perfect for me this child
Whose small imperfect limits would keep breaking:
Within new limits now, arrange the world
Within our walls, within our golden ring.

MICHAEL LONGLEY (b 1939)

Epithalamion

These are the small hours when
Moths by their fatal appetite
That brings them tapping to get in,
Are steered along the night
To where our window catches light.

Who hazard all to be
Where we, the only two it seems,
Inhabit so delightfully
A room it bursts its seams
And spills on to the lawn in beams,

Such visitors as these
Reflect with eyes like frantic stars
This garden's brightest properties,
Cruising its corridors
Of light above the folded flowers,

Till our vicinity
Is rendered royal by their flight
Towards us, till more silently
The silent stars ignite,
Their aeons dwindling by a night,

And everything seems bent
On robing in this evening you
And me, all dark the element
Our light is earnest to,
All quiet gathered round us who,

When over the embankments
A train that's loudly reprobate
Shoots from silence into silence,

With ease accommodate
Its pandemonium, its freight.

I hold you close because
We have decided dark will be
For ever like this and because,
      My love, already
The dark is growing elderly.

      With dawn upon its way,
Punctually and as a rule,
The small hours widening into day,
      Our room its vestibule
Before it fills all houses full,

      We too must hazard all,
Switch off the lamp without a word
For the last of night assembled
      Over it and unperturbed
By the moth that lies there littered,

      And notice how the trees
Which took on anonymity
Are again in their huge histories
      Displayed, that wherever we
Attempt, and as far as we can see,

      The flowers everywhere
Are withering, the stars dissolved,
Amalgamated in a glare,
      Which last night were revolved
Discreetly round us – and, involved,

      The two of us, in these
Which early morning has deformed,
Must hope that in new properties
      We'll find a uniform
To know each other truly by, or,

      At the least, that these will,
When we rise, be seen with dawn
As remnant yet part raiment still,
      Like flags that linger on
The sky when king and queen are gone.

AIDAN CARL MATHEWS (b 1956)

Two Months Married

We can tell already
The history of chips in the skirting,
Hammer-marks at the towel-rail,
Or why the asparagus fern
Is housed in the cooking pot
With the hairline crack.

Today, I was cleaning
With the wrong cloth as you hid
Photographs behind photographs.

On the kitchen window there,
Natural Crystal Salt
Flared in a gust of sun;

The marked-down Sage and Mint
From the Nile's source
Unstoppered their genies.

In a room facing south,
A tree-house with the ladder drawn up,
We're home even as we set out.

Foodstore and software,
A clearing and a hideaway in which
We two may be together and alone

With a radio left on
Always, talking of envoys
Going back to a bombed city.

LAMENTATION

ANONYMOUS (9th-10th century)

The Lament of Créide the Daughter of Gúaire for Her Lover, Dínerteach

(from the Irish, translated by Eoin Neeson)

Cold are the nights I cannot sleep,
Thinking of my love, my dear,
Of the nights we spent together,
Myself and my love from Roigne.

This terrible love for one from afar,
A lord of men, has placed a bar
Upon my youth – (my grief is deep)
And in the nights I cannot sleep.

No music sweeter than his tongue
Save that of heaven's adoration:
Flame that held no word of boasting
Slender, gentle, tender lover.

When I was just a little girl
The burning of my flesh was still:
But in my womanhood I find
Wantonness beguiles my mind.

By Kilcolman's sloping lands,
Where Limerick lies 'neath Aidne's hands,
Men still praise a noble flame,
Dínerteach, that was his name.

His death, dear Christ, torments my heart –
It cannot be that we're apart:
These arrows in their cruel flight
Drive sleep from every bitter night.

ANONYMOUS (9th-12th century)

Fand's Lamentation When About to Leave Cuchulain
(from the Irish, translated by Eleanor Hull)

It is I who must go on this journey,
Our great necessity were best for me;
Though another should have an equal fame
Happier for me could I remain.

Happier it were for me to be here,
Subject to thee without reproach,
Than to go – though strange it may seem to thee –
To the royal seat of Aed Abrat.

The man is thine, O Emer,
He has broken from me, O noble wife,
No less, the thing that my hand cannot reach,
I am fated to desire it.

Many men were seeking me
Both in shelters and in secret places;
My tryst was never made with them,
Because I myself was high-minded.

Joyless she who gives love to one
Who does not heed her love;
It were better for her to be destroyed:
If she be not loved as she loves.

With fifty women hast thou come hither,
Noble Emer, of the yellow locks
To overthrow Fand, it were not well
To kill her in her misery.

Three times fifty have I there
– Beautiful, marriageable women –
Together with me in the fort:
They will not abandon me.

MURROUGH O'DALAIGH (12th-13th century)

On the Death of His Wife

(from the Irish, translated by Frank O'Connor)

I parted from my life last night,
    A woman's body sunk in clay:
The tender bosom that I loved
    Wrapped in a sheet they took away.

The heavy bosom that had lit
    The ancient boughs is tossed and blown;
Hers was the burden of delight
    That long had weighed the old tree down.

And I am left alone tonight
    And desolate is the world I see
For lovely was the woman's weight
    That even last night had lain on me.

Weeping I look upon the place
    Where she used to rest her head –
For yesterday her body's length
    Reposed upon you too, my bed.

Yesterday that smiling face
    Upon one side of you was laid
That could match the hazel bloom,
    In its dark, delicate, sweet shade.

Maelva of the shadowy brows
    Was the mead-cask at my side;
Fairest of all flowers that grow
    Was the beauty that has died.

My body's self deserts me now,
    The half of me that was her own,
Since all I knew of brightness died
    Half of me lingers, half is gone.

The face that was like hawthorn bloom
    Was my right foot and my right side;
And my right hand and my right eye
    Were no more mine than hers who died.

Poor is the share of me that's left
    Since half of me died with my wife;
I shudder at the words I speak;
    Dear God, that girl was half my life.

And our first look was her first love;
    No man had fondled 'ere I came
The little breasts so small and firm
    And the long body like a flame.

For twenty years we shared a home,
    Our converse milder with each year;
Eleven children in its time
    Did that tall stately body bear.

It was the King of hosts and roads
    Who snatched her from me in her prime:
Little she wished to leave alone
    The man she loved before her time.

Now King of churches and of bells,
    Though never raised to pledge a lie
That woman's hand – can it be true? –
    No more beneath my head will lie.

ANONYMOUS (17th-19th century)

Song (*from the Irish, translated by Thomas MacDonagh*)

The stars stand up in the air,
The sun and the moon are gone,
The strand of its waters is bare,
And her sway is swept from the swan.

The cuckoo was calling all day,
Hid in the branches above,
How my stóirín is fled far away –
'Tis my grief that I give her my love!

Three things through love I see,
Sorrow and sin and death –
And my mind reminding me
That this doom I breathe with my breath.

But sweeter than violin or lute
Is my love, and she left me behind –
I wish that all music were mute,
And I to my beauty were blind.

She's more shapely than swan by the strand,
She's more radiant than grass after dew,
She's more fair than the stars where they stand –
'Tis my grief that her ever I knew.

GEORGE OGLE (?1742-1814)

Mailligh Mo Stór

As down by Banna's banks I strayed,
    One evening in May,
The little birds, in blithest notes,
    Made vocal every spray;
They sung their little notes of love,
    They sung them o'er and o'er.
Ah! grádh mo chroídhe, mo cailín og,
    'Si Mailligh mo stór.

The daisy pied, and all the sweets
    The dawn of Nature yields –
The primrose pale, and violet blue,
    Lay scattered o'er the fields;
Such fragrance in the bosom lies
    Of her whom I adore.
Ah! grádh mo chroídhe, mo cailín og,
    'Si Mailligh mo stór.

I laid me down upon a bank,
    Bewailing my sad fate,
That doomed me thus the slave of love
    And cruel Molly's hate;
How can she break the honest heart
    That wears her in its core?
Ah! grádh mo chroídhe, mo cailín og,
    'Si Mailligh mo stór.

You said you loved me, Molly dear!
    Ah! why did I believe?
Yet who could think such tender words
    Were meant but to deceive?
That love was all I asked on earth –
    Nay, heaven could give no more.
Ah! grádh mo chroídhe, mo cailín og,
    'Si Mailligh mo stór.

Oh! had I all the flocks that graze
    On yonder yellow hill,
Or lowed for me the numerous herds
    That yon green pasture fill –
With her I love I'd gladly share
    My kine and fleecy store
Ah! grádh mo chroídhe, mo cailín og,
    'Si Mailligh mo stór.

Two turtle-doves, above my head,
    Sat courting on a bough;
I envied them their happiness,
    To see them bill and coo.
Such fondness once for me was shewn,
    But now, alas! 'tis o'er.
Ah! grádh mo chroídhe, mo cailín og,
    'Si Mailligh mo stór.

Then fare thee well, my Molly dear!
    Thy loss I e'er shall moan;
Whilst life remains in my poor heart,
    'Twill beat for thee alone:
Though thou art false, may heaven on thee
    Its choicest blessings pour.
Ah! grádh mo chroídhe, mo cailín og,
    'Si Mailligh mo stór.

EIBHLÍN DHUBH NÍ CHONAILL (?1745-1800)

A Cry for Art O'Leary

(from the Irish, translated by Brendan Kennelly)

White rider of love!

I love your silver-hilted sword
How your beaver hat became you
With its band of gold
Your friendly homespun suit
Revealed your body
Your pin of glinting silver
Glittered in your shirt

On your horse in style
You were sensitive pale-faced
Having journeyed overseas
The English respected you
Bowing to the ground
Not because they loved you
But true to their hearts' hate

They're the ones who killed you
Darling of my heart

My lover
My love's creature
Pride of Immokelly
To me you were not dead
Till your great mare came to me
Her bridle dragging ground
Her head with your startling blood
Your blood upon the saddle
You rode in your prime

I didn't wait to clean it
I leaped across my bed
I leaped then to the gate
I leaped upon your mare
I clapped my hands in frenzy
I followed every sign
With all the skill I knew

Until I found you lying
Dead near a furze bush
Without pope or bishop
Or cleric or priest

To say a prayer for you
Only a crooked wasted hag
Throwing her cloak across you

I could do nothing then
In the sight of God
But go on my knees
And kiss your face
And drink your free blood

My man!
Going out the gate
You turned back again
Kissed the two children
Threw a kiss at me
Saying 'Eileen, woman, try
To get this in order
Do your best for us
I must be going now
I'll not be home again'
I thought that you were joking
You my laughing man
Then you'd have gone free
Rider of the grey eye
And followed them
Who'd murdered me

My man!
I look at you now
All I know of a hero
True man with true heart
Stuck in a coffin
You fished the clean streams
Drank nightlong in halls
Among frank-breasted women

I miss you

My man!

GEORGE DARLEY (1795-1846)

Weep No More! *(To my last Friend – Suzette la Bonne)*

Weep no more, sweet Vevay maiden!
Though my days be o'er,
Sunk to the grave all sorrow-laden,
Prithee weep no more!

Suns shall warm thy cheek as brightly
Though my bed be cold,
Blossoms deck thy brow as lightly
Though they deck my mould:
    Weep not then, fair Vevay maiden!
    Heaven for thee in store
    Keeps my share of joy, dear maiden!
    Prithee weep no more!

Careless willows round me blowing
Shall thy bowers entwine,
Streams by my ear mutely flowing
Shall flow sweet to thine:
    Weep not then, fair Vevay maiden!
    Heaven for thee in store
    Keeps my share of joy, dear maiden!
    Prithee weep no more!

Winds that rave my burial ditty
Shall thy minstrels be,
Eyes that pass me without pity
Shall go worship thee:
    Weep not then, fair Vevay maiden!
    Heaven for thee in store
    Keeps my share of joy, dear maiden!
    Prithee weep no more!

Thou shalt be by loves attended
I have never known,
To my foreign tomb attended
By thy tears alone!
    Weep not then, fair Vevay maiden!
    Heaven for thee in store
    Keeps my share of joy, dear maiden!
    Prithee weep no more!

OSCAR WILDE (1854-1900)
Hélas!

To drift with every passion till my soul
Is a stringed lute on which all winds can play,
Is it for this that I have given away
Mine ancient wisdom, and austere control?
Methinks my life is a twice-written scroll
Scrawled over on some boyish holiday
With idle songs for pipe and virelay,
Which do but mar the secret of the whole.
Surely there was a time I might have trod
The sunlit heights, and from life's dissonance
Struck one clear chord to reach the ears of God:
Is that time dead? Lo! with a little rod
I did but touch the honey of romance –
And must I lose a soul's inheritance?

FRANCIS LEDWIDGE (1891-1917)
The Death of Ailill

When there was heard no more the war's loud sound,
And only the rough corncrake filled the hours,
And hill winds in the furze and drowsy flowers,
Maeve in her chamber with her white head bowed
On Ailill's heart was sobbing: 'I have found
The way to love you now,' she said, and he
Winked an old tear away and said: 'The proud
Unyielding heart loves never.' And then she:
'I love you now, though once when we were young
We walked apart like two who were estranged
Because I loved you not, now all is changed.'
And he who loved her always called her name
And said: 'You do not love me; 'tis your tongue
Talks in the dusk; you love the blazing gold
Won in the battles, and the soldier's fame.

You love the stories that are often told
By poets in the hall.' Then Maeve arose
And sought her daughter Findebar: 'Oh, child,
Go tell your father that my love went wild
With all my wars in youth, and say that now
I love him stronger than I hate my foes ...'
And Findebar unto her father sped
And touched him gently on the rugged brow,
And knew by the cold touch that he was dead.

LORNA REYNOLDS (b 1911)

Euridyce

Ah, the shining castle over the water
That rose to my sight
Softly bright,
As you me, apostate from deity,
Exile from the orb of light,
Led back from the long occlusion of the night,
You Orpheus, me Euridyce.

My heavy hand travelled along the rainbow
And dabbed in marble sparks;
At the end of my lashes
Suns hung swinging on every blink;
My fingers glowed ruby-red, as me,
Up the long tunnel from night to day, you led
You Orpheus, me Euridyce.

Your flute split petals beneath my feet;
In links of flowers I stepped.
Cowslip-sweet the breath
Blown down the dazzling southern-facing shaft,
As we climbed and wound from dusky underground,
Up far on the way, you leading me
You Orpheus, me Euridyce.

O, Orpheus, farewell: for now we part.
I turn at the mouth
Of the way.
And you me, apostate from deity.
Exile from the orb of light,
Send back to the long occlusion of the night.
Oh, Orpheus! Your lost Euridyce.

HUGH MAXTON (b 1947)

Sonnet at King's Cross *from* Formal Lament

Orpheus did not come and who am I
On stepped flame, surviving, incompetent?
Regarding the finest eye since Egypt
Looking at the ancient eye which is now
Among the optional gods most constant.
Now with blazing throat touch the unaddressed,
With distant throat in my Self comforted
In the absolute process *d'escalier.*

Tendance, again, tendance, you give to me
Most violable spirit. And the bird sing
And the humming kitchen of the spirit
Where I must walk in momentary being.
Allowed to think of you absent in life
Restful, unquiet, the brow arched in sleep.

PARTINGS
&
RETURNINGS

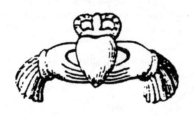

ANONYMOUS (9th century)

Liadain *(from the Irish, translated by Frank O'Connor)*

Gain without gladness
Is the bargain I have struck;
One that I loved I wrought to madness.

Mad beyond measure
But for God's fear that numbed her heart
She that would not do his pleasure.

Was it so great
My treason? Was I not always kind?
Why should it turn his love to hate?

Liadain,
That is my name, and Cuirithir
The man I loved; you know my sin.

Alas too fleet!
Too brief my pleasure at his side;
With him the passionate hours were sweet.

Woods woke
About us for a lullaby,
And the blue waves in music spoke.

And now too late
More than for all my sins I grieve
That I turned his love to hate.

Why should I hide
That he is still my heart's desire
More than all the world beside?

A furnace blast
Of love has melted down my heart,
Without his love it cannot last.

ANONYMOUS (13th-17th century)

I Shall Not Die for You

(from the Irish, translated by Padraic Colum)

Woman, shapely as the swan,
On your account I shall not die,
The men you've slain – a trivial clan –
Were less than I.

I ask me shall I die for these,
For blossom-teeth and scarlet lips?
And shall that delicate swan-shape
Bring me eclipse?

Well-shaped the breasts and smooth the skin,
The cheeks are fair, the tresses free;
And yet I shall not suffer death,
God over me!

Those even brows, that hair like gold,
Those languorous tones, that virgin way;
The flowing limbs, the rounded heel
Slight men betray.

Thy spirit keen through radiant mien,
Thy shining throat and smiling eye,
Thy little palm, thy side like foam –
I cannot die!

O woman, shapely as the swan,
In a cunning house hard-reared was I;
O bosom white, O well-shaped palm,
I shall not die.

ANONYMOUS (?16th century)

Song at Parting (from the Irish,
translated by the Earl of Longford)

Now, since of this alone I'm sure,
That you were false to me,
Do you endure and I'll endure
That we should strangers be.

So if you chance to hear my name
In cottage or in hall,
Speak neither praise of me nor blame,
Nor talk of me at all.

And if we meet, as we may do,
At church or on the plain,
You'll pass me by as I will you,
Nor turn your head again.

We'll ne'er admit that it was I
That did you so adore,
And both of us will soon deny
We even met before.

ANONYMOUS (18th-19th century)

The Colleen Rue

As I roved out one summer's morning, speculating most curiously,
To my surprise, I soon espied a charming fair one approaching me;
I stood awhile in deep meditation, contemplating what should I do,
But recruiting all my sensations, I thus accosted the Colleen Rue:

'Are you Aurora, or the beauteous Flora, Euterpasia, or Venus bright?
Or Helen fair, beyond compare, that Paris stole from her
      Grecian's sight?
Thou fairest creature, you have enslaved me, I am intoxicated by
      Cupid's clue,
Whose golden notes and infatuation deranged my ideas for you,
      Colleen Rue.'

'Kind sir, be easy, and do not tease me, with your false praise so jestingly,
Your dissimulations and invitations, your fantastic praises, seducing me.
I am not Aurora, or the beauteous Flora, but a rural maiden to
    all men's view,
That's here condoling my situation, and my appellation is the
    Colleen Rue.'

'Was I Hector, that noble victor, who died a victim of Grecian skill,
Or was I Paris, whose deeds were various, as an arbitrator on Ida's Hill,
I would roam through Asia, likewise Arabia, through Pennsylvania
    seeking you,
The burning regions, like famed Vesuvius, for one embrace of the
    Colleen Rue.'

'Sir, I am surprised and dissatisfied at your tantalising insolence,
I am not so stupid, or enslaved by Cupid, as to be dupèd by your
    eloquence,
Therefore desist from your solicitations, I am engaged, I declare it's true,
To a lad I love beyond all earthly treasures, and he'll soon embrace
    his Colleen Rue.'

WILLIAM CONGREVE (1670-1729)

Song

> False though she be to me and love,
>   I'll ne'er pursue revenge;
> For still the charmer I approve,
>   Though I deplore her change.
>
> In hours of bliss we oft have met,
>   They could not always last;
> And though the present I regret,
>   I'm grateful for the past.

SIR RICHARD STEELE (1672-1729)

Why, Lovely Charmer, Tell Me Why

Why, lovely charmer, tell me why,
So very kind, and yet so shy?
Why does that cold forbidding air
Give damps of sorrow and despair?
Or why that smile my soul subdue,
And kindle up my flames anew?

In vain you strive with all your art,
By turns to freeze and fire my heart;
When I behold a face so fair,
So sweet a look, so soft an air,
My ravished soul is charmed all o'er,
I cannot love thee less nor more.

MÍCHÉAL MacRUADHRAIGHE (18th-19th century)

The Little Yellow Road

(from the Irish, translated by Joseph Campbell)

I am sick, sick,
No part of me sound;
The heart in my middle
Dies of its wound,
Pining the time
When she did stand
With me shoulder to shoulder
And hand in hand.

I travelled west
By the little yellow road
In the hope I might see
Where my Secret abode.
White were her two breasts,
Red her hair,
Guiding the cow
And the weaned calf, her care.

Until wind flows
From this stream west,
Until green plain spreads
On the withered crest,
And white fields grow
The heather above,
My heart will not find
Kindness from my love.

There's a flood in the river
Will not ebb till day,
And dread on me
That my love is away.
Can I live a month
With my heart's pain
Unless she will come
And see me again?

I drink a measure
And I drink to you,
I pay, I pay,
And I pay for two.
Copper for ale
And silver for beer –
And do you like coming
Or staying here?

THOMAS MOORE (1779-1852)

To ——

When I loved you, I can't but allow
I had many an exquisite minute;
But the scorn that I feel for you now
Hath even more luxury in it!

Thus, whether we're on or we're off,
Some witchery seems to await you;
To love you is pleasant enough
And oh! 'tis delicious to hate you!

ANONYMOUS (?19th century)

The Lapful of Nuts

(from the Irish, translated by Sir Samuel Ferguson)

Whene'er I see soft hazel eyes
    And nut-brown curls,
I think of those bright days I spent
    Among the Limerick girls;
When up through Cratla woods I went,
    Nutting with thee;
And we plucked the glossy clustering fruit
    From many a bending tree.

Beneath the hazel boughs we sat,
    Thou, love, and I,
And the gathered nuts lay in thy lap,
    Beneath thy downcast eye:
But little we thought of the store we'd won,
I, love, or thou;
For our hearts were full, and we dare not own
    The love that's spoken now.

Oh, there's wars for willing hearts in Spain,
    And high Germanie!
And I'll come back, 'ere long, again,
    With knightly fame and fee:
And I'll come back, if I ever come back,
    Faithful to thee,
That sat with thy white lap full of nuts
    Beneath the hazel tree.

ISABELLA VALANCY CRAWFORD (1850-1887)

We Parted in Silence

We parted in silence, we parted by night,
    On the banks of that lonely river;
Where the fragrant limes their boughs unite,
    We met – and we parted forever!
The night-bird sung, and the stars above
    Told many a touching story,
Of friends long passed to the kingdom of love,
Where the soul wears its mantle of glory.

We parted in silence – our cheeks were wet
    With the tears that were past controlling;
We vowed we would never, no, never forget,
    And those vows at the time were consoling;
But those lips that echoed the sounds of mine
    Are as cold as that lonely river;
And that eye, that beautiful spirit's shrine,
    Has shrouded its fires forever.

And now on the midnight sky I look,
    And my heart grows full of weeping;
Each star is to me a sealéd book,
    Some tale of that loved one keeping.
We parted in silence – we parted in tears,
    On the banks of that lonely river:
But the odour and bloom of those bygone years
    Still hang o'er its waters forever.

LADY AUGUSTA GREGORY (1852-1932)

Wild Words I Write

Wild words I write, wild words of love and pain
To lay within thy hand before we part,
For now that we may never meet again
I would make bare to thee my inmost heart.
For when I speak you answer with a jest
Or laugh and break the sentence with a kiss
And so my love is never half confessed
Nor have I told thee what has been my bliss.
And when the darkness and the clouds prevail
And I begin to know what I have lost
I would not vex thee with so sad a tale
Or tell how all too dear my love has cost.
    But now the time has come when I must go
    The tumults and the joy I fain would show.

KATHARINE TYNAN (1861-1931)

Not Lovers Then

Not lovers then but friends
Until our world's glimpse ends
    Dear, take my hand on this;
Since you have willed it so
    I am content you know
    Let's part without a kiss.

For love is full of smart
To wound and break a heart
    The heart it sets to beat
Even[r] so; your words are wise
Look once into my eyes
    Was not the old way sweet?

Let the old love lie there
With hidden face and hair.
        While you and I forget
So dead and piteous
He will not trouble us
        Making our eyes wet.

JOHN MILLINGTON SYNGE (1871-1909)

Abroad

Some go to game, or pray in Rome
I travel for my turning home
For when I've been six months abroad
Faith your kiss would brighten God!

WINIFRED M. LETTS (1882-1950)

If Love of Mine

If love of mine could witch you back to earth
It would be when the bat is on the wing,
The lawn dew-drenched, the first stars glimmering,
The moon a golden slip of seven nights' birth.
If prayer of mine could bring you it would be
To this wraith-flowered jasmine-scented place
Where shadow trees their branches interlace;
Phantoms we'd tread a land of fantasy.
If love could hold you I would bid you wait
Till the pearl sky is indigo and till
The plough show silver lamps beyond the hill
And Aldebaran burns above the gate.
If love of mine could lure you back to me.

FRANCIS STUART (b 1902)

Homecoming

By plane, bus and forced march
Across a city after midnight
With nothing to guide me but what you'd called
Your candelit window amid the electric ones
(But the phone was cracked and the tone was poor.
And perhaps I hadn't heard aright).
I reached a house and struck a light
To read what was chalked beside the bell:
'Once for the Captain, twice for Sue'.
Three times I pressed;
Give me a minute to catch my breath
Before you open, whoever you are.

RHODA COGHILL (b 1903)

Flight

This is the road that since the summer – since
their parting – she shunned, for fear of meeting him.
 Until the time of ripening their quarrel
 lasted, and in September, when the harvest
was brimming in the fields, she went her way
by other paths. Through any opening gate
 he suddenly might come, on a waggon loaded
 with tousled grain; and when mists of a mild October
crawled on the sodden soil, he would be cutting
his straggled hedges, time-serving till the sullen
 fallow land should harden with more than the first
 gossamer frost, and open to winter work.

But today she takes that road in the late afternoon
when already across the bloodshot sky the rooks
    are blinking home. She is no longer afraid while
    the year lasts, knowing the watchdog daylight
whines in November on a shortened leash.
She holds her scarf tightened along her cheek;
    her worn shoes make no noise but a crisp soft
    crushing of frozen grass and ivy and dock,
that keep her footsteps, still as a pattern in damask.
She moves in the ditch of the drab lane, patched with agate
    ice-pools, dried after sharp showers by a long
    sweeping wind. Her ears tell that beyond
the sheltering hedge two horses – a stubble-dappled
roan, and a mare as red as springing sally
    whips or a burnt-out beech – are treading the dead-branch
    crumbling clay, that breaks against the metal
harrow's teeth ... He shouts to make them turn;
behind him turns a cloud of white sea-birds ...

She keeps to the near ditch; but the road winding
and bending again shows a new-made breach in the briars.
    At the treacherous gap she stops. Oh! now to run,
    to hide like a feathered frightened thing in the dusk!
But she who thought to pass like a bird or a bat,
encountering only the hedge-high gulls, is trapped;
    for the too-familiar face, the known shape
    walking the furrows, are seen ... So it was vain
to shield evasive eyes, to discipline
rebellious feet: vain to her and to him
    the fugitive pretence. For a proud pulse
    beats in her brain like a startled wing; the blood
tramples its path in the stubborn heart's field
with the eightfold stamping hooves of a strong team
    of horses; and she feels, raking the flesh,
    the harrow of love's remembered violence.

ANNE LE MARQUAND HARTIGAN (b 1931)

Salt

.I would not write a lament for you:
A requiem for you, a song for you,
I would not twine a remembrance for you,
I do not think sweetly of you, of your
Past kindness, past pleasures, past lies.

I am not biding my time for you, not repining
For you, you cause me no more the sleepless nights.
For I have killed you. I have dried you up.
Anger I have for you.
With anger I have washed out pain.
Sweet healing anger opening my eyes on you.
Seeing you, without the love blur in them.
Tears now pillars of salt,

Could call curses on you, spit on you,
Laugh at you, but I just smile at you,
Leave you alone. Climbed free of you
Away from the power of you the hold of you
The grip of you the hurt of you from
Feeding the need of you, filling you.

Bringing gifts to you. Bringing strengths
To you. I turn my power on you,
I shine that fierce light on you, you cannot
Move or run, Caught in my full beam
Only I can unleash this moving thing.
You cannot understand it you cannot know it
But you can feel it under your brain;
Rabbit you, caught in my glare.

Clear of you, clean of you
Swept of you, no more bereft of you,
My kisses not for you
No words for you
No sweet looks for you
No look over my shoulder for you.
Turn my heel on you, my back to you.
I have no lack of you. It is you
That is to be pitied now.

RICHARD WEBER (b 1932)

Stephen's Green Revisited

The spring sun bends down between the branches.
The ducks continue with their cry of aqua, aqua.
Last autumn we came here for a little silence,
Our toes tempting the water, a breath of breeze
Hardly disturbing us; talked and were silent.
As in a picture, with everyone stopped in the act
Of moving or looking, a minute became an instant,
The world suddenly stilled in a midday haze of sun.
Even the ducks were silent, their bodies unmoving
Over unmoving reflections. Then slowly the world
Began to go again, and time helped us to our feet.
The ducks quickly recalled their little Latin
And their work of furrowing waves in the water.
Later your brown eyes watched me leave you sadly
But hopefully. Six months have passed since then
And we have said goodbye again in another city.
We have everything to hope for, yet I write sadly.
Memory is the mother of the muses, someone said.
But sadness is surely the secret mother of memory.

MEDBH McGUCKIAN (b 1950)

The Aphrodisiac

She gave it out as if it were
A marriage or a birth, some other
Interesting family event, that she
Had finished sleeping with him, that
Her lover was her friend. It was his heart
She wanted, the bright key to his study,
Not the menacings of love. So he is
Banished to his estates, to live
Like a man in a glasshouse; she has taken to
A little cap of fine white lace
In the mornings, feeds her baby
In a garden you could visit blindfold
For its scent alone:
                        But though a ray of grace
Has fallen, all her books seem as frumpish
As the last year's gambling game, when she
Would dress in pink taffeta, and drive
A blue phaeton, or in blue, and drive
A pink one, with her black hair supported
By a diamond comb, floating about
Without panniers. How his most
Caressing look, his husky whisper suffocates her,
This almost perfect power of knowing
More than a kept woman. The between-maid
Tells me this is not the only secret staircase.
Rumour has it she's taken to rouge again.

MAURA DOOLEY (b 1957)

And I'll Get Back to You as Soon as I Can

I listen to you tell why
You are not there, then dial
Again to have your voice
Unspool inside me, one more time
My calls to you, like a shoal
Of little wishes, replay
As clicks and silences in
The flood of business messages.

ÁINE NÍ GHLINN (b 1958)

The Broken Step

(from the Irish, translated by Gabriel Fitzmaurice)

I hear you when you climb the stairs. You walk
on the broken step. Everyone else avoids it, but
you walk on it always.

You asked me what my name was. We were together
and you said my eyes were blue.

If you see sunlight at nightfall and if
it awakens a poem in you ...
    That's my name.

If you visit me and I know it's you
because I hear your footstep on the stair ...
    That's my name.

You said you understood and that my eyes were blue.
You walked again on it when you left this morning.

You come into the room and I see from your eyes that
you were with her. You do not speak nor do you look
into my eyes. Her fragrance flows from you.

The fragrance is slender, tall, well-formed, and her
hair is long and curling. I hear you tell her that her
eyes are blue and that you love her.

I open the door and you walk out.
You can explain you tell me. I close
    the door.

You do not walk on it. You avoid the broken step.
No-one walks on the broken step. They avoid it
always.

SINÉAD O'CONNOR (b 1966)

The Last Day of Our Acquaintance

This is the last day of our acquaintance
I will meet you later in somebody's office
I'll talk but you won't listen to me
I know what your answer will be

I know you don't love me anymore
you used to hold my hand when the plane took off
two years ago there just seemed so much more
and I don't know what happened to our love

Today's the day
our friendship has been stale
and we will meet later to finalise the details
two years ago the seed was planted
and since then you have taken me for granted

You were no life-raft to me
I drowned in pain and misery
you did nothing to stop me
now drown in your own self-pity

But this is the last day of our acquaintance
I will meet you later in somebody's office
I'll talk but you won't listen to me
I know your answer already

CELEBRATION

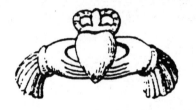

THOMAS MOORE (1779-1852)
Oh, Call It by Some Better Name

Oh, call it by some better name,
For Friendship sounds too cold,
While Love is now a worldly flame,
Whose shrine must be of gold;
And Passion, like the sun at noon,
That burns o'er all he sees,
Awhile as warm, will set as soon –
Then, call it none of these.

Imagine something purer far,
More free from stain of clay
Than Friendship, Love or Passion are,
Yet human still as they:
And if thy lip, for love like this,
No mortal word can frame,
Go, ask of angels what it is,
And call it by that name.

EDWARD DOWDEN (1843-1913)
Waking

Waking is wonder; summer airs
    Ripple the wheat-field, where a crew
Of winged sweet thieves in flights, in pairs,
    Their knavish craft pursue.

They dip, lurk, eddy, swing and sway
    Upon the stalk – glad, wrangling throats;
While silent to the wind-flecked bay
    Glide home the pilchard-boats.

Waking is infant joy new born;
    And how should wonder e'er be dead
For me, who lean toward the morn
    Across so dear a head?

HERBERT TRENCH (1865-1923)

Come, Let Us Make Love Deathless

Come, let us make love deathless, thou and I,
    Seeing that our footing on the Earth is brief –
Seeing that her multitudes sweep out to die
    Mocking at all that passes their belief.
For standard of our love not theirs we take;
    If we go hence to-day
Fill the high cup that is so soon to break
    With richer wine than they!

Ay, since beyond these walls no heavens there be
    Joy to revive or wasted youth repair,
I'll not bedim the lovely flame in thee
    Nor sully the sad splendour that we wear.
Great be thy love, if with the lover dies
    Our greatness past recall,
And nobler for the fading of those eyes
    The world seen once for all!

JOHN MILLINGTON SYNGE (1871-1909)

Is It a Month

Is it a month since I and you
In the starlight of Glen Dubh
Stretched beneath a hazel bough
Kissed from ear and throat to brow,
Since your fingers, neck, and chin
Made the bars that fenced me in,
Till Paradise seemed but a wreck
Near your bosom, brow, and neck,
And stars grew wilder, growing wise,
In the splendour of your eyes!
Since the weasel wandered near
Whilst we kissed from ear to ear

And the wet and withered leaves
Blew about your cap and sleeves,
Till the moon sank tired through the ledge
Of the wet and windy hedge?
And we took the starry lane
Back to Dublin town again.

DEREK MAHON (b 1941)

Two Songs

His Song
Months on, you hold me still;
at dawn, bright-rising, like a hill-
horizon, gentle, kind with rain
and the primroses of April.
I shall never know them again
but still your bright shadow
puts out its shadow, daylight, on
the shadows I lie with now.

Her Song
A hundred men imagine
love when I drink wine;
and then I begin to think
of your words and mine.
The mountain is silent now
where the snow lies fresh,
and my love like the sloe-
blossom on a blackthorn lies.

NUALA NÍ DHOMHNAILL (b 1952)

Destiny

(from the Irish, translated by Paul Muldoon)

All those summer evenings in Ballinloosky (it was never
more than one evening, perhaps)
we're young, in love, without two pennies to rub together,
and we while away the hours by taking alternate sips
from a single, solitary pint. The bay's so overcast,
what with a heat-haze, that the oil-tankers and factory-ships
laboriously making their way past
gravely and gloriously salute each other
with three long boom-blasts.

Down at the Poll Gorm, the whoops of youngsters and teens
as they gallivant through the waves into which they've hurled
themselves. The droning on and on
of passers-by with time to kill and not a care in the world.
Our first major quarrel, when you announce
that you've found, in the kitchen, a talking blackbird.
'A talking blackbird? Stuff and nonsense. Absolute baloney.'
And we're snapping and sniping away for ages until it dawns
on me it's not a 'blackbird' but a 'mynah'

which is a 'black bird', yes indeed.
Such little matters of stress lead to major stress and strain:
we're just getting to know each other and pay no heed
to the 'vast culture-gap' and the 'ne'er the twain ...'
We imagine that this happiness can last for ever and ever,
that all's hunky-dory, that nothing can come between
us to break the spell: we're sitting on a bench by an aviary
in a beer-garden; from the lawn a blackbird incites
a riot of finches and spurs them on to higher and yet again
     higher

trebles and trills .... In Ballinloosky this long, hot summer,
little do we know that storm clouds loom on the horizon
and that we'll soon be enmeshed in vile rumours.
Our enemies are even now tightening their seines.
We're oblivious of the cruel trough
into which we'll sink. For destiny's a black cat with designs
on me from under the impending elder-bush: its claws
    unsheathed
and its eyes aglow, it'll make one lithe, limber,
lethal attack. My exultant singing spirit. My ululations of grief.

PLEASURE

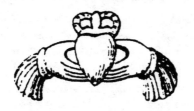

ANONYMOUS (9th century)

The Lovely Étan
(from the Irish, translated by Thomas Kinsella)

I don't know who it is
that Étan is going to sleep with.
But I know the lovely Étan
will not be sleeping alone.

ANONYMOUS (18th century)

Dear Dark Head
(from the Irish, translated by Sir Samuel Ferguson)

Put your head, darling, darling, darling,
    Your darling black head my heart above;
Oh, mouth of honey, with the thyme for fragrance,
    Who, with heart in breast, could deny you love?

Oh, many and many a young girl for me is pining,
    Letting her locks of gold to the cold wind free,
For me, the foremost of our gay young fellows;
    But I'd leave a hundred, pure love, for thee!

Then put your head, darling, darling, darling,
    Your darling black head my heart above;
Oh, mouth of honey, with the thyme for fragrance,
    Who, with heart in breast, could deny you love?

OSCAR WILDE (1854-1900)

The Harlot's House

We caught the tread of dancing feet,
We loitered down the moonlit street,
And stopped beneath the harlot's house.

Inside, above the din and fray,
We heard the loud musicians play
The 'Treues Liebes Herz' of Strauss.

Like strange mechanical grotesques
Making fantastic arabesques,
The shadows raced across the blind.

We watched the ghostly dancers spin
To sound of horn and violin,
Like black leaves wheeling in the wind.

Like wire-pulled automatons,
Slim silhouetted skeletons
Went sidling through the slow quadrille.

They took each other by the hand,
And danced a stately saraband;
Their laughter echoed thin and shrill.

Sometimes a clockwork puppet pressed
A phantom lover to her breast,
Sometimes they seemed to try to sing.

Sometimes a horrible marionette
Came out, and smoked its cigarette
Upon the steps like a live thing.

Then, turning to my love, I said,
'The dead are dancing with the dead,
The dust is whirling with the dust.'

But she – she heard the violin,
And left my side, and entered in:
Love passed into the house of lust.

Then suddenly the tune went false,
The dancers wearied of the waltz,
The shadows ceased to wheel and whirl.

And down the long and silent street,
The dawn, with silver-sandalled feet,
Crept like a frightened girl.

WILLIAM BUTLER YEATS (1865-1939)

His Memories

We should be hidden from their eyes,
Being but holy shows
And bodies broken like a thorn
Whereon the bleak north blows,
To think of buried Hector
And that none living knows.

The women take so little stock
In what I do or say
They'd sooner leave their cosseting
To hear a jackass bray;
My arms are like the twisted thorn
And yet there beauty lay;

The first of all the tribe lay there
And did such pleasure take –
She who had brought great Hector down
And put all Troy to wreck –
That she cried into this ear,
'Strike me if I shriek.'

E. R. DODDS (1893-1979)

When the Ecstatic Body Grips

When the ecstatic body grips
Its heaven, with little sobbing cries,
And lips are crushed on hot blind lips,
I read strange pity in your eyes.

For that in you which is not mine,
And that in you which I love best,
And that, which my day-thoughts divine
Masterless still, still unpossessed,

Sits in the blue eyes' frightened stare,
A naked lonely-dwelling thing,
A frail thing from its body-lair
Drawn at my body's summoning;

Whispering low, 'O unknown man,
Whose hunger on my hunger wrought,
Body shall give what body can,
Shall give you all – save what you sought.'

Whispering, 'O secret one, forgive,
Forgive and be content though still
Beyond the blood's surrender live
The darkness of the separate will.

'Enough if in the veins we know
Body's delirium, body's peace –
Ask not that ghost to ghost shall go,
Essence in essence may cease.'

But swiftly, as in sudden sleep,
That You in you is veiled or dead;
And the world's shrunken to a heap
Of hot flesh strained on a bed.

FREDA LAUGHTON

When to My Serene Body

When to my serene body yours
Leans in a quiet ecstasy
And coolly our limbs
Seek their several felicity,
The skin with its silken kiss
Moves creamily over skin
Into a dream that is
A tower of the skin's thought;
Your body melting to mine,
Cool and warm at once
And water-smooth, in the sun's
Long amorous ardour caught.

In its own need pursuing,
Skin, the body's chess,
In a separate loveliness,
Along belly and thigh and breast
Sinks in its long caress.

LOUIS MacNEICE (1907-1963)

from **Trilogy for X**

And love hung still as crystal over the bed
    And filled the corners of the enormous room;
The boom of dawn that left her sleeping, showing
    The flowers mirrored in the mahogany table.

O my love, if only I were able
    To protract this hour of quiet after passion,
Not ration happiness but keep this door for ever
    Closed on the world, its own world closed within it.

But dawn's waves trouble with the bubbling minute,
    The names of books come clear upon their shelves,
The reason delves for duty and you will wake
    With a start and go on living on your own.

The first train passes and the windows groan,
    Voices will hector and your voice become
A drum in tune with theirs, which all last night
    Like sap that fingered through a hungry tree
Asserted our one night's identity.

EITHNE STRONG (b 1923)

Immutable

I wait
because you have not told me.

And all night I dream of your mouth
and of the slow essence of your body.

I am awake to the song of you
and I sing.

The slow white dream of you.

I know my flesh calls you in;
my eyes hold you;
the dark thrall I have for you
is about you.

You will not go
unspoken.

The years will see.

PAUL DURCAN (b 1944)

Making Love outside Áras an Uachtaráin

When I was a boy, myself and my girl
Used bicycle up to the Phoenix Park;
Outside the gates we used lie in the grass
Making love outside Áras an Uachtaráin.

Often I wondered what de Valera would have thought
Inside in his ivory tower
If he knew that we were in his green, green grass
Making love outside Áras an Uachtaráin.

Because the odd thing was – oh how odd it was –
We both revered Irish patriots
And we dreamed our dreams of a green, green flag
Making love outside Áras an Uachtaráin.

But even had our names been Diarmaid and Gráinne
We doubted de Valera's approval
For a poet's son and a judge's daughter
Making love outside Áras an Uachtaráin.

I see him now in the heat-haze of the day
Blindly stalking us down;
And, levelling an ancient rifle, he says 'Stop
Making love outside Áras an Uachtaráin.'

NUALA NÍ DHOMHNAILL (b 1952)

Without Your Clothes (from the Irish, translated by Paul Muldoon)

Though I much prefer you / minus
your clothes / – your silk shirt / and your
tie / your umbrella tucked under the
oxter / and your three-piece suit / tailored in
sartorial elegance.

Your shoes which always sport / a high shine / your
doe-skin gloves / on your hands / your crombie
hat / tipped elegantly over the ear – / none of
them add / a single whit to your presence.

For underneath them / unbeknownst to all / is a
peerless body / without blemish or fault / the litheness
of a wild animal / a great nocturnal cat / prowling
and leaving destruction / in its wake.

Your broad strong shoulders / and your skin / as
smooth as windblown snow / on the mountainside /
Your back, your slender waist / and in your
crotch / that growing root / that is pleasure's very source.

Your complexion so dark / and soft / as silk with the
pile of velvet / in its weave / and smelling very much of
meadowsweet / or watermead, as it is called / that
they say has power / to lead men and women astray.

Therefore, and for that reason / when you go dancing
with me tonight / though I would prefer you stark naked /
by my side / I suppose you had better / put your
clothes on / rather than have half the women
of Ireland / totally undone.

RITA ANN HIGGINS (b 1955)

It's Platonic

It's platonic
Platonic my eye,

I yearn
for the fullness
of your tongue
making me
burst forth
pleasure after pleasure
after dark

Soaking all my dream

THE
SUPERNATURAL

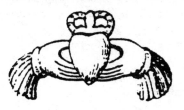

WILLIAM ALLINGHAM (1824-1889)
The Witch-Bride

A fair witch crept to a young man's side,
And he kissed her and took her for his bride.

But a Shape came in at the dead of night,
And filled the room with snowy light.

And he saw how in his arms there lay
A thing more frightful than mouth may say.

And he rose in haste, and followed the Shape
Till morning crowned an eastern cape.

And he girded himself, and followed still
When sunset sainted the western hill.

But, mocking and thwarting, clung to his side,
Weary day! – the foul witch-bride.

ETHNA CARBERY (1846-1870)
The Love-Talker

I met the Love-Talker one eve in the glen,
He was handsomer than any of our handsome young men,
His eyes were blacker than the sloe, his voice sweeter far
Than the crooning of old Kevin's pipes beyond in Coolnagar.

I was bound for the milking with a heart fair and free –
My grief! my grief! that bitter hour drained the life from me;
I thought him human lover, though his lips on mine were cold,
And the breath of death blew keen on me within his hold.

I know not what way he came, no shadow fell behind,
But all the sighing rushes swayed beneath a fairy wind;
The thrush ceased its singing, a mist crept about,
We two clung together – with the world shut out.

Beyond the ghostly mist I could hear my cattle low,
The little cow from Ballina, clean as driven snow,
The dun cow from Kerry, the roan from Inisheer,
Oh, pitiful their calling – and his whispers in my ear!

His eyes were a fire; his words were a snare;
I cried my mother's name, but no help was there;
I made the blessed Sign – then he gave a dreary moan,
A wish of cloud went floating by, and I stood alone.

Running ever through my head is an old-time rune –
'Who meets the Love-Talker must weave her shroud soon.'
My mother's face is furrowed with the salt tears that fall,
But the kind eyes of my father are the saddest sight of all.

I have spun the fleecy lint and now my wheel is still,
The linen length is woven for my shroud fine and chill,
I shall stretch me on the bed where a happy maid I lay –
Pray for the soul of Máire Óg at dawning of the day!

OLIVER ST JOHN GOGARTY (1878-1959)

Begone, Sweet Ghost

Begone, sweet Ghost, O get you gone!
Or haunt me with your body on;
And in that lovely terror stay
To haunt me happy night and day.
For when you come I miss it most,
Begone, sweet Ghost!

But do not clothe you in the dress
Whereby was young Actaeon killed;
He died because of loveliness,
And I will die from that withheld,
Unless you take on flesh, unless
In that you dress!

YOUTH
AGE
&
MEMORY

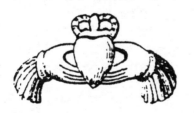

ANONYMOUS (7th-12th century)

The Woman of Beare (from the Irish, translated by Stephen Gwynn)

Ebbing, the wave of the sea
Leaves, where it wantoned before
Wan and naked the shore,
Heavy the clotted weed.
And in my heart, woe is me!
Ebbs a wave of the sea.

I am the Woman of Beare.
Foul am I that was fair,
Gold-embroidered smocks I had,
Now in rags am hardly clad.

Arms, now so poor and thin,
Staring bone and shrunken skin,
Once were lustrous, once caressed
Chiefs and warriors to their rest.

Not the sage's power, nor lone
Splendour of an agèd throne,
Wealth I envy not, nor state.
Only women folk I hate.

On your heads, while I am cold,
Shines the sun of living gold.
Flowers shall wreathe your necks in May:
For me, every month is grey.

Yours the bloom: but ours the fire,
Even out of dead desire.
Wealth, not men, ye love; but when
Life was in us, we loved men.

Fair the men, and wild the manes
Of their coursers on the plains;
Wild the chariots rocked, when we
Raced by them for mastery.

Lone is Femen: vacant, bare,
Stands in Bregon Ronan's Chair.
And the slow tooth of the sky
Frets the stones where my dead lie.

The wave of the great sea talks:
Through the forest winter walks.
Not to-day by wood and sea
Comes King Diarmuid here to me.

I know what my king does.
Through the shivering reeds, across
Fords no mortal strength may breast,
He rows – to how chill a rest!

Amen! Time ends all.
Every acorn has to fall.
Bright at feasts the candles were,
Dark is here the house of prayer.

I, that when the hour was mine
Drank with kings the mead and wine,
Drink whey-water now, in rags
Praying among shrivelled hags.

Amen! Let my drink be whey,
Let me do God's will all day –
And, as upon God I call,
Turn my blood to angry gall.

Ebb, flood, and ebb; I know
Well the ebb: and well the flow,
And the second ebb, all three –
Have they not come home to me?

Came the flood that had for waves
Monarchs, mad to be my slaves,
Crested as by foam with bounds
Of wild steeds and leaping hounds.

Comes no more that flooding tide
To my silent dark fireside.
Guests are many in my hall,
But a hand has touched them all.

Well is with the isle that feels
Now the ocean backward steals:
But to me my ebbing blood
Brings again no forward flood.

Ebbing, the wave of the sea
Leaves, where it wantoned before,
Changed past knowing the shore,
Lean and lonely and grey.
And far and farther from me
Ebbs the wave of the sea

ANONYMOUS (18th century)
The Coughing Old Man

Each female so pretty in country and city,
I pray you will pity a languishing maid,
That is daily vexed and nightly perplexed,
All by my old husband – I wish he were dead.
He's cross grained and crooked and doating stupid,
And has no more sense than a young sucking calf,
Although he lies by me he ne'er can enjoy me,
For still when he is noodling he is killed with the cough.

The very first night that he came to bed to me,
I longed for a trial at Venus's game,
But to my sad vexation and consternation,
His hautboy was feeble and weak in the main.
For instead of pleasing he only kept teasing;
To him then I turned my back in a huff,
But still he did cry, 'twill do by-and-by,
A *chusla se sthere!* I am killed with the cough.

This doating old creature a remnant of nature,
His shins are so sharp as the edge of a knife,
His knees they are colder than snow on a mountain,
He stands more in need of a nurse than a wife;
I by him sit weeping whilst he lies a-sleeping,
Like a hog in a sty he does grunt and puff,
A wheezing and harking both sneezing and farting,
And worse than all that he's killed with the cough.

His breath it does stink like asafoetadu,
His blobbring and slobbring I can't bear,
For each night when I lie beside him,
He must have a spitting cup placed on his chair;
His nose and his chin are joined together,
His tawny old skin is yellow and tough,
Both trembling and shaking like one in the ague,
Still smothering and spitting and killed with the cough.

For sake of cursed money my father has undone me,
By making me wed this doating old man,
Although some might shame me what Maid can blame me,
To crown him with horns as soon as I can;
What signifies treasure without any pleasure,
I'm young and would have enjoyed enough,
And not to be tied to a gouty old fellow,
That's withered and worn and killed with the cough.

Since fortune to me has proved so cruel,
In brief my intention to you I'll relate
If he does not alter and fare the better,
No longer on him I mean to wait.
I'll have a look out for some rousing young fellow,
That's able to give me some reason to laugh;
If such I can find then I'll swap my old cuckold,
And pitch to the vengeance himself and his cough.

ANONYMOUS (18th-19th century)

The Old Man of Kilcockan

(from the Irish, translated by Donal O'Sullivan)

By prayer and entreaty and threat they did worry me
To be wed to the gaffer my youth denied.
On leaden feet to the priest they did hurry me,
With a heart stone dead while the knot was tied.
I like not his gait nor the rheumy red eyes of him,
His furry grey brows, the groans and the sighs of him,
I long for a young man to lie and to rise with him,
Who would kiss and caress me at morning tide!

All maids yet unwed, whether wealthy or dowerless,
Be warned by my fortune against old drones,
For I lie by a dotard both shrivelled and powerless,
As good to possess as a heap of bones.
Wide-eyed each night, with a heart that's like lead in me.
I think of the withered old creature that's wed to me.
Compared to the stalwart that might lie abed with me,
Clasping me to him with love's sweet tones!

Six guineas I'd give, and I'd pay it right readily,
If someone would put my old man away,
Come on him by stealth and take aim at him steadily,
Make sure of the target and earn his pay:
Or if in the sea he could set about drowning him,
Lay him flat in the ditch and knock the wall down on him.
Or perhaps better still just to throttle the jowl of him
And leave him for dead just before the day!

Last night as I lay between waking and sleeping
I heard that my wretched old man was dead.
I leapt from the pillow, my gratitude heaping
On the man in the ditch who had done the deed
They made up their story while still there was breath in him,
'Twas the bay mare that kicked him – and that was the
      death of him.
Go take to the young man this news that is best for him –
In the grave at Kilcockan my wretch is laid!

ANONYMOUS (?18th century)

Youth and Age *(from the Irish, translated by Eleanor Hull)*

> Once I was yellow-haired, and ringlets fell,
>   In clusters round my brow;
> Grizzled and sparse tonight my short grey crop,
>   No lustre in it now.
>
> Better to me the shining locks of youth,
>   Or raven's dusky hue,
> Than drear old age, which chilly wisdom brings,
>   If what they say be true.
>
> I only know that as I pass the road,
>   No woman looks my way;
> They think my head and heart alike are cold –
>   Yet I have had my day.

WILLIAM BUTLER YEATS (1865-1939)

After Long Silence

> Speech after long silence; it is right,
> All other lovers being estranged or dead,
> Unfriendly lamplight hid under its shade,
> The curtains drawn upon unfriendly night,
> That we descant and yet again descant
> Upon the supreme theme of Art and Song:
> Bodily decrepitude is wisdom; young
> We loved each other and were ignorant.

ANONYMOUS (date unknown)

Light Love *(from the Irish, translated by Robin Flower)*

Out of sight is out of mind,
Maids no loyal faith maintain;
Light love goes ranging and always changing
Like a shifting April's sun and rain.

You were mine a year ago,
Love this year is fled away;
And that bright weather we knew together
Is clouded over since yesterday.

Ne'er a woman loves me now,
And my loving days are done;
That one should leave me it does not grieve me,
But women turn from me, everyone!

DENIS DEVLIN (1908-1959)

from **The Colours of Love**

At the *Bar du Départ* drink farewell
And say no word you'll be remembered by;
Nor Prince nor President can ever tell
Where love ends or when it does or why.

Down the boulevard the lights come forth
Like my rainflowers trembling all through Spring,
Blue and yellow in the Celtic North ...
The stone's ripple weakens, ring by ring.

Better no love than love, which, through loving
Leads to no love. The ripples come to rest ...
Ah me! how all that young year I was moving
To take her dissolution to my breast!

PÁDRAIG Ó SNODAIGH (b 1935)

from **From Parnell to Queenie** *(from the Irish, translated by Gabriel Fitzmaurice)*

Paris
I have no pictures of you now
I didn't keep the few you left me:
notes ... a handful of scraps ...
fraying to powder at the edges
fading
on the age-stained folds.

But you are always before me
like that apt word on the tip of the tongue
that doesn't come
– a certain expression on faces
that turn the inquisitive head
... where did I see that before?
on whom?
your voice with one woman
your walk with another
... the flurry of an entrance
... the hat askew
your neck before me, your back,
your hands raising a cup.
You are vanishing
bit by bit
like broken glass smoothed
in the roll of the sea.

And I thought ... isn't it the same
with the relics of the saints,
a tooth here,
this one's clothes, that one's handkerchief, yet another's pen.

And then I realised that I'm a relic of you,
my hair you ran your fingers through
my lips where you laid your mouth.

You didn't fall with the white flakes of your letters
I tore up on the Pont Neuf.
The river didn't swallow you along with them.
You last while I do.

INDEX OF POEM TITLES

INDEX OF FIRST LINES

INDEX OF FIRST LINES

INDEX OF AUTHORS, TRANSLATORS AND POEMS

INDEX OF AUTHORS, TRANSLATORS AND POEMS

INDEX OF AUTHORS, TRANSLATORS AND POEMS

ACKNOWLEDGMENTS

I have greatly appreciated the help of several friends, Professor Warwick Gould, Professor Brendan Kennelly, Professor Colin Smythe, Dr Bruce Stewart, Dr Loreto Todd and Dr Peter Van de Kamp. I am also very grateful to Dr Andrew Carpenter for drawing my attention (in a lecture he delivered on early eighteenth-century popular poetry at Carrickfergus Castle in November 1996) to two poems I have included here, 'On Deborah Perkins of the County of Wicklow' and 'The Coughing Old Man'; these will appear in his *Verse in English from Eighteenth-Century Ireland* to be published by Cork University Press in 1998.

Grateful acknowledgement is made to the following for their permission to reprint the poems in this book. All possible care has been taken to trace copyright and make full acknowledgements. If any errors or omissions have occurred, please notify the publishers and corrections will be made in subsequent editions.
AE [George Russell]: 'The Burning Glass' courtesy of Colin Smythe Ltd; **Fergus Allen:** 'Age Twelve' and 'The Fall' courtesy of the author; **Leland Bardwell:** 'Lullaby' courtesy of the author; **Samuel Beckett:** 'I Would Like my Love' reprinted with permission of Calder Publications Ltd; **George Buchanan:** 'Song for Straphangers' courtesy of Sandra Buchanan; **Eavan Boland:** 'Song' from An Origin Like Water: Collected Poems 1967-1987 by Eavan Boland. Copyright © 1996 by Eavan Boland. Reprinted by permission of W W Norton & Company, Inc., New York and Carcanet Press, London; **Rosita Boland:** 'Fireworks' courtesy of the author; **Dermot Bolger:** 'Stardust' courtesy of the author and A P Watt Ltd; **Joseph Campbell:** translation of 'The Little Yellow Road' courtesy of Simon Campbell; **Austin Clarke:** 'Celibacy', 'The Straying Student', and the translation of 'Mabel Kelly' courtesy of R Dardis Clarke of 21 Pleasants Street, Dublin 8; **Brian Coffey:** 'The Nicest Phantasies are Shared' courtesy of John Coffey; **Padraic Colum:** translations of 'I Shall Not Die for Thee' and 'The Poor Girl's Meditation' courtesy of the Estate of Padraic Colum; **Cecil Day-Lewis:** 'Now She is Like the White-Tree Rose' courtesy of Sinclair Stevenson; **Maura Dooley:** 'And I'll get back to You as Soon as I Can' courtesy of the author and Bloodaxe Books; **Denis Devlin:** extract from 'The Colour of Love' courtesy of The Dedalus Press; **E R Dodds:** 'When the Ecstatic Body Grips' courtesy of the Estate of E R Dodds; **Theo Dorgan:** 'All Souls' Eve' courtesy of the author; **Paul Durcan:** 'Hymn to a Broken Marriage', 'Making Love outside Áras an Uachtaráin' and 'The Levite and his Concubine at Gibeah' from his collection A Snail in my Prime. First published in Great Britain in 1993 by Harvill. © Paul Durcan. Reproduced by permission of The Harvill Press; **Andrew Elliott:** 'Eavesdropping' courtesy of the author; **Padraic Fallon:** 'The River Walk' and 'Women' from Collected Poems (1993), by kind permission of the Estate of Padraic Fallon, The Gallery Press and Carcanet Press; **Gabriel Fitzmaurice:** translations of 'Entreaty' by Caitlín Maude, 'The Broken Step' by Áine ní Ghlinn and 'From Parnell to Queenie' by Pádraig Ó Snodaigh; **Robin Flower:** translations of 'Light Love' and 'Proud Lady' courtesy of The Lilliput Press, Dublin; **Monk Gibbon:** 'Song' courtesy of the executors; **Oliver St John Gogarty:** 'Begone, Sweet Ghost' courtesy of Oliver D Gogarty SC; **Lady Augusta Gregory:** translation of Antoine Ó Raifterai's 'Mary Hynes of Baile-laoi' and 'Wild Words I Write' courtesy of Colin Smythe Ltd; **Seamus Heaney:** 'A Dream of Jealousy' from Fieldwork by Seamus Heaney. Copyright © 1981 by Seamus Heaney. 'Poem for Marie' from Selected Poems 1965-1975 by Seamus Heaney. Copyright © 1980 by Seamus Heaney. Reprinted by permission of Faber & Faber, London, and Farrar, Straus & Giroux, Inc. New York; **F R Higgins:** 'O, You Among Women' and courtesy of Alice Higgins; **Rita Ann Higgins:** 'It's Platonic' courtesy of the author and Salmon Press; **Douglas Hyde:** translations of 'The Coolun', 'The Red Man's Wife', 'My Love, Oh, She is My Love' courtesy of Douglas Sealy; **Earl of Longford:** translations of 'Against Blame of Women', 'The Kiss' and 'Song at Parting' by kind permission of the executors; **Patrick Kavanagh:** 'Bluebells of Love' by kind permission of the Trustees of the Estate of Patrick Kavanagh, c/o Peter Fallon, Literary Agent, Loughcrew, Oldcastle, Co Meath, Ireland; **Brendan Kennelly:** translations of 'Cry for Art O'Leary', 'Hate Goes Just as Far as Love', 'A Love-Song' and for 'We are Living' courtesy of Brendan Kennelly; **Thomas Kinsella:** translations of 'The Lovely Étan' and 'Úna Bhán' and 'In the Ringwood' courtesy of the author; **Anne Le Marquand Hartigan:** 'Salt' courtesy of the author and Salmon Press; **James Liddy:** 'History' reprinted with permission from Collected Poems. © 1994 by The Creighton University Press. **Michael Longley:** 'Epithalamion' courtesy of the author; **Joan McBreen:** 'This Moon, These Stars' courtesy of the author; **Patrick MacDonogh:** 'Be Still as You are Beautiful' courtesy of the Estate of Patrick MacDonogh; **Medbh McGuckian:** 'The Aphrodisiac' by kind permission of the author and The Gallery Press; **Louis MacNeice:** 'Coda' and extract from 'Trilogy for X' courtesy of David Higham Associates; **Derek Mahon:** 'The Lost Girls' and 'Two Songs' courtesy of the author; **Aidan Carl Mathews:** 'Two Months Married' by kind permission of the author and The Gallery Press; **Caitlín Maude:** 'Entreaty' courtesy of Cathal Ó Luain; **Hugh Maxton:** 'Sonnet at King's Cross' courtesy of the author; **John Montague:** 'Crossing' and 'That Room' by kind permission of the author and The Gallery Press; **Paul Muldoon:** translation of 'Destiny' by Nuala ní Dhomhnaill by kind permission of the author and The Gallery Press; **Richard Murphy:** 'Moonshine' courtesy of the author; **Eoin Neeson:** translation of 'The Lament of Créide the Daughter of Gúaire for Her Lover, Dínerteach' from Poems for the Irish by Eoin Neeson, Mercier 1966, Ward River Press 1985; **Eiléan ní Chuilleanáin:** translation of 'Lay Your Arms Aside' courtesy of the translator; **Nuala ní Dhomhnaill:** 'Destiny', 'Labasheedy' and 'Without Your Clothes' courtesy of the author; **Áine ní Ghlinn:** 'The Broken Step' courtesy of the author; **Frank O'Connor:** translations of 'Liadain' and 'On the Death of His Wife', 'She is My Dear' courtesy of the O'Donovan Trust; **Sinead O'Connor:** 'The Last Day of Our Acquaintance' © 1990 EMI Music Pub (Holland) BV, UK. EMI Music Publishing Ltd, London WC2H OEA. Reproduced by permission of International Music Publications Ltd; **Mary O'Malley:** 'Aftermath' courtesy of the author; **Pádraig Ó Snodaigh:** 'Paris' from From Parnell to Queenie courtesy of the author; **Lorna Reynolds:** 'Eurydice' courtesy of the author; **W R Rodgers:** 'Stormy Night' courtesy of The Gallery Press; **James Simmons:** 'A Song' courtesy of the author; **James Stephens:** 'Nóra Críona' and 'The Daisies' courtesy of the Society of Authors; **Eithne Strong:** 'Dedication' and 'Immutable' courtesy of the author and Salmon Press; **LAG Strong:** 'The Brewer's Man' reprinted by permission of The Peters Fraser and Dunlop Group Limited; **Francis Stuart:** 'Homecoming' courtesy of the author; **Arland Ussher:** translation of 'Against Clerical Celibacy' by Brian Merriman courtesy of Josef Keith and Mrs Gerald Staples; **William Butler Yeats:** translation of 'After Long Silence' reprinted with the permission of Simon & Schuster from The Collected Works of W. B. Yeats, Volume 1: The Poems, revised and edited by Richard J. Finneran. Copyright 1933 by Macmillan Publishing Company; copyright renewed © 1961 by Bertha Georgie Yeats; 'His Memories' and extract from The Gift of Harun Al-Rashid reprinted with the permission of Simon & Schuster from The Collected Works of W B Yeats, Volume 1: The Poems, revised and edited by Richard J. Finneran. Copyright 1928 by Macmillan Publishing Company; copyright renewed © 1956 by Georgie Yeats. 'He Wishes for the Cloths of Heaven' and 'No Second Troy' reprinted with permission of Simon Schuster from The Collected Works of W. B. Yeats, Volume 1: The Poems, revised and edited by Richard J. Finneran (New York:Macmillan, 1989); also reprinted with permission of A P Watt Ltd on behalf of Michael Yeats.